TAFF VALE RAILWAY *Miscellany*

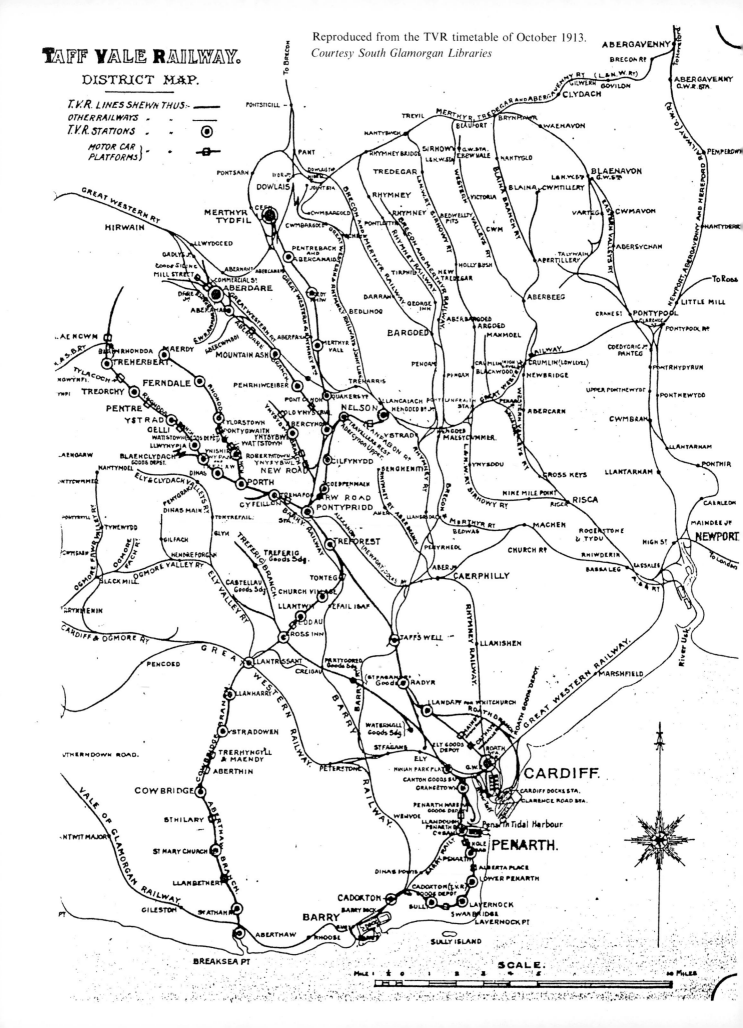

TAFF VALE RAILWAY Miscellany

John Hutton

Oxford Publishing Co.

Dedication

My daughters Nicola and Joanna, who carried my camera and accompanied me on my railway walks.

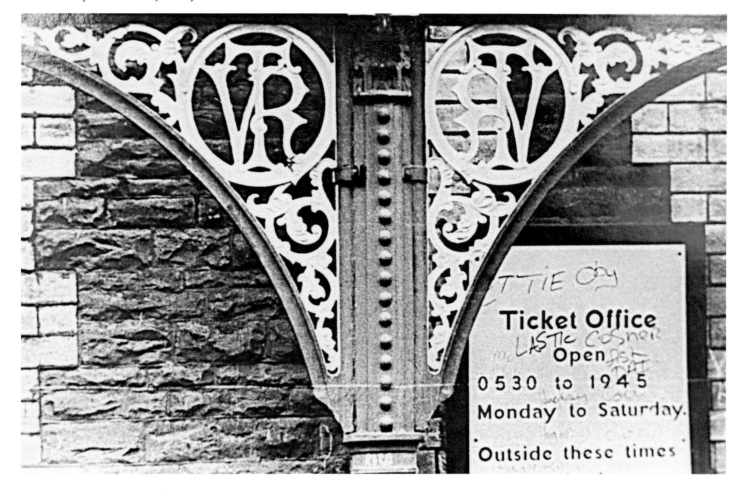

A FOULIS-OPC Railway Book

Published by:
Haynes Publishing Group
Sparkford, Near Yeovil, Somerset. BA22 7JJ

Haynes Publications Inc.
861 Lawrence Drive, Newbury Park, California 91320, USA.

Printed by J.H. Haynes & Co.

British Library Cataloguing in Publication Data
Hutton, John
    Taff Vale miscellany.
    1. Wales. South Wales. Railway services.
    Taff Vale Railway.
    I. Title.
    385.09429'4
    ISBN 0-860932-414

Publisher's note: A number of the photographs in this album are from original prints of poor quality, but have been included because of their rarity and historical interest and importance.

Introduction

The origins of the Taff Vale Railway Company can be traced back many years to 1804. In that year Richard Trevithick, a Cornishman, drove a steam locomotive of his own design for a bet, down the Merthyr tramroad to Abercynon which was then called Navigation House, a distance of some 10 miles.

This tramway was used by horse power to take iron products from the iron works at Merthyr and Dowlais to be shipped to Cardiff Docks via the Glamorganshire Canal. It was found that the locomotive designed by Trevithick was too heavy for the rails but it was decided that the expense involved to re-lay the tramway with heavier rails was just not justified. Therefore the TVR came into being because colliery owners like Coffin, Insole, Gethin and others were finding it more and more difficult to supply their customers with a quick delivery of good steam coal. Their tramways to the Glamorganshire Canal at Pontypridd were just not adequate to keep pace with the increase in demand. The ironmasters of Merthyr and Dowlais were also faced with these same problems, so on the 21st of June 1836, the Taff Vale Railway received Royal Assent, and a young engineer called Mr Isambard Kingdom Brunel was appointed to survey for the best route available.

The Taff Vale Railway became one of the most prosperous railways in the kingdom. The main line was from Cardiff Docks to Merthyr and from this 24 mile line there were no less than 23 branch lines making a total of 124 miles 42 chains, of Taff Vale Railway ownership. Although built through mountainous country there were only two tunnels, one at Ynysycol near Taffs Well, and the other on the notorious incline between the area of Abercynon and Quakers Yard. They were both opened out into cuttings in 1862 when the main line was doubled.

The busiest junction of the system was at Pontypridd, with a train passing every two minutes, and passenger trains running to places like Treherbert, Maerdy, Ynysybwl, Nelson, Aberdare, Caerphilly, Llantrisant, Cowbridge and Aberthaw, as well as Cardiff and Merthyr. In the early days of the TVR there were three rope worked inclines; Abercynon to Incline Top, near Quakers Yard, Dowlais Junction to the Dowlais Iron works, near Merthyr, and Pwllyrhebog to Blaenclydach, near Tonypandy. This last mentioned incline was worked by specially designed engines right up to July 1951.

Engine sheds had an aroma of their own, a blend of steam, heat and hot oil, of which there were twelve of them scattered around the Taff Vale system. The coaching stock was large and varied, and catered for three classes of travel. These coaches had dark chocolate coloured lower panels, with white upper panels, while workmens' carriages were dark brown all over.

The stations, except those at Cardiff, Pontypridd and Treherbert were simple in design, yet functional in every way. Three stations had lifts, Cardiff Queen Street, from street level to platforms, as at Pontypridd, but Tonypandy was unique in as much as the lift worked from the 'up' platform, to street level, and was hydraulically worked by using water from the adjacent river.

Signal boxes were also unique in design, and only at Abercwmboi, Llandaff, and Radyr Quarry are Taff Vale boxes still in existence today. Goods depots were at most stations with the largest being at Merthyr and Pontypridd, where every type of traffic was handled. Cattle pens existed at Llandaff, Pontypridd, Merthyr, Ystrad Rhondda and Treorchy, as well as Aberdare and Tonypandy.

The Taff Vale Railway made good use of the docks at Cardiff and also Penarth, where the best of Welsh coal was shipped to all over the world. Today, most of the former branch lines of this great company have now disappeared. Some were dismantled years ago and yet most can still be followed, through areas that have become lost in the growing blanket of nature, and the modern day estates of houses and factories. The lines that are still in use have changed, sidings have been lifted as the collieries were closed, and superfluous lines removed.

I have tried "through the lens of the camera", to capture the past and illustrate the changes that have occurred, and to show how things used to be, for present day youngsters to compare scenes of their local "down the road station", where the ivy has crept onto broken platform slabs or the sleepers, now broken and rotten, with just a scattering of ballast faintly noticeable amongst the weeds and grass, showing a trace of the track. If my work kindles an interest for them to find out more about their local history and to ask "why" then I have achieved my aim.

British Rail has started building new stations and halts on those lines that are still operational. Some are at the planning stage and some have actually been built. As new housing and factory estates are extended so British Rail has tried to recapture the spirit of the past and provide a service for the public and to regain lost revenue. Perhaps they will also realise that instead of selling the former branch lines to the property developers, they would do better to reopen these lines and provide a service not only to the new estates, but to the old villages, once again.

John A Hutton
Pontypridd.

Mr I.K. Brunel, FRS engineer, deposited on the night, at the time of half past eleven, on the 30th of November in the year of 1835, with the Clerk of the Peace, of the County of Glamorgan, the completed, surveyed plans for the directors of the Taff Vale Railway Company, eventually resulting in the Royal Assent by His Gracious Majesty, King William IV, to the Act of Parliament, of the 21st of June 1836.

Letter stamps, printed in sheets of twelve (three rows of four). First printed in January 1891 and available until 1897.

Courtesy J.C. Hayden

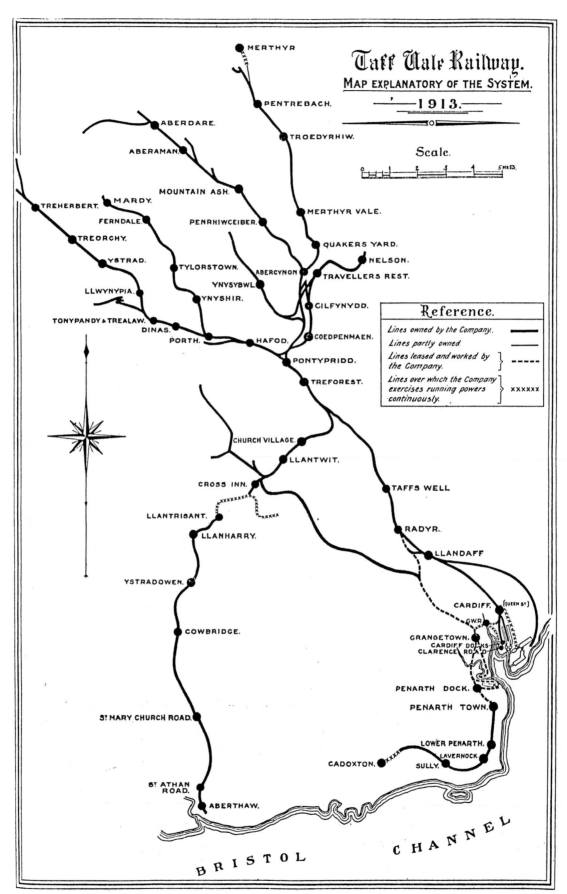

Taff Vale Railway.
MAP EXPLANATORY OF THE SYSTEM.
— 1913. —

Scale.

Reference.

Lines owned by the Company.
Lines partly owned.
Lines leased and worked by the Company.
Lines over which the Company exercises running powers continuously.   XXXXXX

MERTHYR
PENTREBACH.
TROEDYRHIW.
ABERDARE.
ABERAMAN.
MOUNTAIN ASH.
MERTHYR VALE.
TREHERBERT.   MARDY.
FERNDALE.   PENRHIWCEIBER.
QUAKERS YARD.
TREORCHY.   NELSON.
YSTRAD.   TYLORSTOWN.   ABERCYNON.   TRAVELLERS REST.
YNYSYBWL.
LLWYNYPIA.   YNYSHIR.   CILFYNYDD.
TONYPANDY & TREALAW.   COEDPENMAEN.
DINAS.
PORTH.   HAFOD.   PONTYPRIDD.
TREFOREST.

CHURCH VILLAGE.
LLANTWIT.
CROSS INN.   TAFFS WELL.
XXXXXXXXX
LLANTRISANT.   XXXXX
LLANHARRY.   RADYR.
LLANDAFF.
YSTRADOWEN.
CARDIFF.   (QUEEN ST)
GWR
COWBRIDGE.   GRANGETOWN.
CARDIFF DOCKS.
CLARENCE ROAD.
PENARTH DOCK.
PENARTH TOWN.
ST MARY CHURCH ROAD.
LOWER PENARTH.
LAVERNOCK.
CADOXTON.   XXXXX   SULLY.
ST ATHAN ROAD.
ABERTHAW.

BRISTOL   CHANNEL

A brief summary of the twenty three branches owned by The Taff Vale Railway Company.
(Total 124 miles 42 chains.)

Aberdare Branch, runs along the valley of the Cynon river, from Abercynon to Bwllfa Dare, total $10^1/2$ miles.

Aberthaw Branch, stretches from Cowbridge to Aberthaw, total $6^1/2$ miles.

Cadoxton Branch, runs from Penarth to Biglis Junction, total $4^1/2$ miles.

Cowbridge Branch, from Llantrisant to Cowbridge, total $5^3/4$ miles.

Cwmbach Branch, near Abercwmboi in the Aberdare Valley, total $^1/2$ mile.

Dowlais Pits Branch, between Stormstown and Abercynon, total $^1/2$ mile.

East Branch, along the east side of West Bute Dock, total $^3/4$ mile.

Eirw (or Aerw) Branch, stretches from Hafod to Cymmer, in the Rhondda Valley, total $^3/4$ mile.

Llancaiach Branch, from Stormstown to Nelson and Llancaiach, to connect with the junction there, with the GWR, total $3^1/4$ miles.

Llandaff Loop, a connecting line that joins the main line and the Penarth line at Llandaff, total 29 chains.

Llantrisant Branch, runs from Treforest to Llantrisant, where it forms a junction with the GWR line, total $5^1/4$ miles.

Llantrisant Common Branch, from Cross Inn to a junction with the GWR line, in the Ely Valley, near Coedely, total $2^1/2$ miles.

Llantrisant No. 1 Branch, from Cross Inn to Waterhall Junction, near to Llandaff, total 7 miles.

Penarth Branch, runs from Radyr to Penarth Dock and Penarth Town, total 7 miles.

Penarth Harbour Branch, stretches from Grangetown, a part of Cardiff, to the Penarth Harbour, total $1^1/2$ miles.

Pont Shon Norton Branch, (and Cilfynydd Loop) runs along the eastern side of the Taff Valley, between Abercynon and Pontypridd, total $2^1/2$ miles.

Pwllyrhebog Branch, from Tonypandy to Clydach Vale, total 2 miles.

Rhondda Branch, along the valley of the Rhondda Fawr river, stretching from Pontypridd to Blaenrhondda, total $12^3/4$ miles.

Rhondda Fach Branch, runs along the valley of the Rhondda Fach river, from Porth to Maerdy, total 6 miles.

Roath Branch, from Llandaff to Roath Dock at Cardiff, total 5 miles.

Treferig Branch, runs along the valley of the Mychydd river to the Glyn Colliery, total $2^3/4$ miles.

Ynysfach Branch, a short stretch which runs from Merthyr goods yard to the Cyfarthfa Ironworks, total $^1/2$ mile.

Ynysybwl Branch, runs along the valley of the Clydach river, from Stormstown to the parish district of Llanwonno, total 6 miles.

Destination label, below and parcels labels, right.

Courtesy J.Morgan

Taff Vale Railway.
YSTRAD
TO
PENCADER
G.W.
Via TREHERBERT & BRITON FERRY

FROM
The Forest Iron and Steel Co., Limited,
TREFOREST, T.V.R.

Taff Vale Railway
CARDIFF, QUEEN STREET
TO
Quakers Yard

The Main Line

The Main line stretched from Cardiff Dock Station, later renamed Bute Road, to Merthyr Plymouth Street Station, and later to the former Vale of Neath Station known as Merthyr High Street. This line followed the course of the Taff river for most of the way and the stations and halts, or platforms as they were originally known, consisted of the following:
Cardiff Bute Road Station, Cardiff West Yard Works, Cardiff Queen Street Station, Cathays Woodville Road Halt, Maindy North Road Halt, Cathays Carriage and Wagon Works, Llandaff Station, Radyr Station, Pentyrch Crossing, Pentyrch Station House, 1st Taffs Well Station, 2nd Taffs Well Station, Treforest Junction, Treforest Goods Depot, Treforest Station, Pontypridd Station, Pontypridd Northern Junction, Pontypridd Goods Depot, Stormstown Sidings, Abercynon Station, Top of the Incline Station, Quakers Yard Low Level Station, Merthyr Vale Station, Treod-y-rhiw Station, Pentrebach Station, Brandy Bridge Junction, Dowlais Junction, Merthyr Junction, Merthyr Plymouth Street Station, Merthyr Viaducts and finally Merthyr High Street Station. Today, only 16 are still in use and the rest are either demolished or are no longer recognisable as to what they once were.

Cardiff Bute Road Station
Known originally as Cardiff Dock Station, this station opened on 8th October 1840, renamed as Cardiff Bute Road Station by the GWR on 1st July 1924, closed for the handling of goods traffic on the 22nd March 1965 but is still in use for passenger services.

Cardiff Dock Station, photographed in June 1921.

B.J. Miller

Cardiff Bute Road Station, 12th September 1951.

H.C. Casserley

Cardiff Queen Street Station

Known originally as Cardiff TVR Station it was opened to all traffic on 8th October 1840, reconstructed in 1887 and renamed Queen Street in the same year. Reconstructed again in 1907 and also in 1973. (Closed to goods traffic on 1st April 1925.)

Queen Street Station yard around or just before 7th June 1886 (The notice on the board invites people to attend a concert to begin on the 7th June 1886 at the Park Hall Cardiff, which was to be attended by the Marquis of Bute.)

Welsh Folk Museum collection

Cardiff Queen Street Station c1900.

Lens of Sutton

Cathays Woodville Road Halt
Known originally as Cathays Woodville Road Platform, it was renamed as Halt by the GWR on the 10th July 1922. Renamed as Woodville Road Halt on the 15th September 1952, the word Cathays being dropped from use. This halt was opened on the 2nd July 1906 and was eventually closed for passenger services on 15th September 1958.

Auto fitted 0-6-0PT No. 6435 passing by Woodville Road Halt on the 28th June 1958.

S. Rickard

Cathays Engine Shed, closed on 30th November 1957.

Aerial photograph of the Cathays Engine Sheds and sidings, looking towards the west, c1927. Note push and pull auto set taking on coal, middle, left of picture.

S. Glamorgan Libraries

Cathays Carriage and Wagon Works

This works was opened in 1845 for the construction and repair of carriages, and eventually ceased in 1905 but since then has concentrated on wagon repairs only.

Cathays Works showing a prefabricated cross-over assembly. Also in view is the old practice of where the sleepers are covered entirely by ballast. Photograph taken around turn of century.

Westrail Enterprises

A look behind the scenes. An inside view of Cathays Wagon Repair Shops 8th June 1983.

British Rail

TAFF VALE RAILWAY.

OLD MATERIAL FOR SALE.

RECEIVED

Answered

TERMS AND CONDITIONS.

1. The intending Purchasers, or their accredited Agents, should view the Material offered, and ascertain for themselves what they are tendering for, as the Company will not be responsible for any error in description.

2. Tenders will be received for the whole or any part of the Materials.

3. Price to be at per ton of 2,240lbs. net cash payment.

4. Payment of the Purchase Money to be made as follows :—25 per cent. of the total amount immediately on acceptance of the Tender, and the balance within two weeks of that date and in advance of delivery.

5. In the event of the Purchaser not making payment within such period, the Company to be at liberty to re-sell the Materials, and the Purchaser to be liable to pay any loss which may result.

6. This Company will load into trucks all Materials sold, and deliver the same free of charge on their Siding at Cardiff or Radyr, as specified herein.

7. The whole of the Materials to be removed off this Company's premises within Four Weeks after the Purchaser has received notice that his Tender is accepted.

8. The Materials are to be unloaded by the Purchaser, and removed or consigned by him from the Siding at which they are delivered, within forty-eight hours of their arrival there, and if not unloaded and removed by that time, the Purchaser will be charged at the usual rate of demurrage on trucks.

9. Should the Purchaser be desirous of sending a person to witness the weighing, due notice will be given to him when the Company are about to weigh the Materials, and he shall not be at liberty to dispute the weight of the same, as declared by the Company, after they have been removed from the Siding at which they were delivered.

10. The Directors do not bind themselves to accept the highest or any Tender, and they reserve to themselves the right to dispose of a portion only of the Articles tendered for.

11. The decision of the Directors will be communicated within seven days from date of Board Meeting, to those Contractors only whose Tenders are accepted.

12. Tenders marked outside, " Tenders for Old Material," will be received on this Form only, if sent by post to the Board of Directors, so as to arrive before 9 a.m. on 5 MAR 1917 191 in the enclosed envelope.

Tenders specifying *Long Weight* will not be entertained.

Taff Vale Railway Offices,
Cardiff.

A. WALKER,
Secretary.

Date, 24 FEB 1917 91

To the Board of Directors of the Taff Vale Railway Company.

We hereby agree to Purchase the Old Materials mentioned in the following *Specification (or any portion thereof), strictly in accordance with the above Terms and Conditions, and at the prices shewn.* MOSS ISAAC

Signed .... *H. Young*

Full Postal Address *122 Cannon Street E.C.*

Dated. *3rd March* 1917

NOTE.—It must be distinctly understood that no tender will be entertained unless made strictly in accordance with the terms contained in this Specification.

No. 4730

DUPLICATE.

(5867)

GREAT WESTERN RAILWAY.

(To be filled in by Chief Engineer's Office.)

NOTE.—It is essential that the utmost economy be exercised in the use of firewood; the allowance made in fulfilment of this application is the ration for the period from July 1st, 1922, to June 30th, 1923.

DIVL. ENGINEER'S OFFICE RECEIVED OCT 18 1922 G.W.R. QUEEN ST., CARDIFF

½ _____ Department.

St. Mary Church Rd Station.

23. 9 _____ 1922

DIVL. ENGINEER'S OFFICE RECEIVED NO. 18 1922

SUPPLY OF FIREWOOD.

Memorandum to H. DEANS, Esq.,

Swindon.

Please supply 25 cwt. of Firewood for lighting fires as under :—

Number of Coal Fires.		Approximate quantity in stock 23.9 1922. cwts.	Previous supplies during winter period 1921-22.	
Lighted daily for which supply is required.	In signal cabins, etc., in continuous use.		Date received.	Amount cwt.
3	-	1	Oct.	25

If there are any special circumstances requiring increased supplies beyond ration give full particulars here.

Signature _____

To W. W. GRIERSON, Esq.,

Kindly arrange supply

H. DEANS

per

Date _____ 192

To DIVISIONAL ENGINEER Cardiff Valle

Please supply 4 cwt. of Firewood to above Station.

4 9/181

Depôt.

for W. W. GRIERSON.

Date 14. 10. 1922

To W. W. GRIERSON, Esq.

Amount supplied 4 cwt.   Date Nov 17 1922

for St Mary Ch Rd

This form to be retained by the Divisional Engineer concerned.

(Form No. T. P. 100.)

2,500 A 24 Spl. 8-22 (2.)

Cardiff Maindy North Road Halt
Known originally as Maindy North Road Platform it was renamed as Maindy North Road Halt on the 10th July 1922. Again renamed, this time as Maindy Halt on the 15th September 1952. This halt opened to passenger services in the May 1907, closing on the 15th September 1958.

Today there is no trace left of this or of Woodville Road Halt.

GWR 0-6-2T No. 5691 on an 'up' valleys passenger service passing Maindy Halt, 25th May 1957.

S. Rickard

Llandaff Station
Opened for passenger and goods services on the 8th October 1840, closing to goods traffic on the 27th June 1966, but it is still in use for passenger services.

Llandaff Station facing towards Maindy direction. Only the main line is still used with all other lines having been lifted. In the background is the former TVR booking office, now closed and covered with graffiti, an unfortunate sign of the times, January 1985.

Author

Radyr Station
Opened (with the closing of Pentyrch Station) in June 1863. Closed to goods traffic on 6th January 1964 but still open for passengers today.

'Up' valleys TVR train passing Radyr Station c1922. The 'up' and 'down' platforms at this station were connected by a footbridge. In November 1983 the 'up' sidings alongside the station were lifted and the area converted into a park and ride car park. Radyr Junction signal box is in the background.

LCGB (Ken Nunn collection)

Radyr Station c1960.

Lens of Sutton

Pentyrch Station
Opened on the 8th October 1840 for passenger services, closed entirely in June 1863.

Pentyrch Station house.
South Glamorgan Libraries

Pentyrch Crossing
Here an early industrial tramroad (which predated the TVR) made a level crossing with the Taff Vale Railway. This private line ran from Melin Griffiths Works to a private siding at Pentyrch and also to a foundry at Taffs Well, known as Pentyrch Foundry. This private line closed in 1962 and the signal box closed the same year.

Pentyrch Crossing c1950.

D.G. Thomas

Taffs Well Station
This second Taffs Well Station has suffered several changes of name, becoming Walnut Tree Junction after the opening of the Rhymney Railway connection in February 1858, then on 1st June 1886, the name was changed to Walnut Tree Bridge. Finally on 16th March 1900 the station was renamed Taffs Well. Closed to goods traffic 27th June 1966 but still in use for passenger.

Overlooking Taffs Well Station, photographed from a train on a South Wales tour that was crossing the former Barry Railway, Walnut Tree Viaduct, 31st July 1965.

D.G. Thomas

Photograph taken in 1904, and includes Taffs Well Station staff, the local vicar, and on the far right Mr Thomas. Note the wooden structure, which was later replaced by bricks left over from the rebuilt Treforest Station.
Courtesy the family of the late Mrs M. Griffiths (née Thomas)

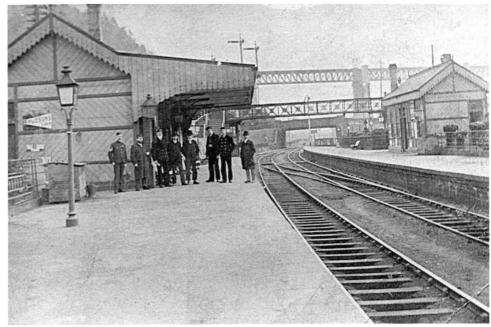

Taffs Well Station, c1960. Photographed when the station buildings had some of the old charm and character left in them. Today these buildings, like most of the former buildings along this line, have been replaced by the more usual 'bus shelters' unfortunately. Note the GWR gas type of lamp, but fitted with a swan neck adapter for electric lighting.

Lens of Sutton

Taffs Well original station house, and the site of the first station photographed on the 6th September 1967. Today this building has become modernised and is almost beyond recognition, compared to when this photograph was taken. (Opened in October 1840)

D. G. Thomas

Trefforest Estate Station, photographed in the August of 1985. Opened by the GWR in 1942, it consisted of an island platform reached by a subway built to serve the workers on the nearby industrial estate, which until a few years ago was a thriving community of factories, but today many are empty buildings.

Author

Treforest Station and Goods Shed (now Trefforest)

Treforest Station was opened in 1847, originally as a halt. The 'down' buildings were destroyed by fire on 18th March 1908 causing the death of a woman. The rebuilt station lasted until 1972, when a modern style waiting room and booking office were built. There were once two junctions at Treforest, the one on the 'down' side being a short-lived connection with the Cardiff Railway. After the ceremonial opening train of 1909 this junction was taken up by the TVR because of a dispute with the Cardiff Railway, who then had to terminate its line on the east side of the impressive viaduct at Rhydyfelin. On the 'up' side and coming down from Tonteg Junction was the Barry Railway spur, opened in 1889, the passenger services ceased travelling over this branch to Llantrisant via Llantwit Fadre in 1952. There are now park and ride facilities at Trefforest, which cover the former relief lines and coal yard sidings.

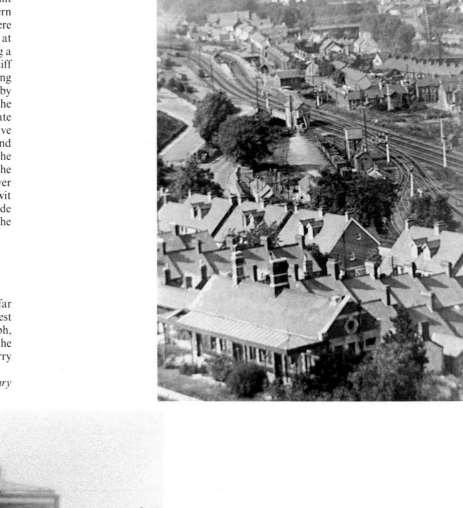

A view of Treforest Station, and in the far background, the sidings and Treforest Junction in the middle of this photograph, taken in 1951. In the foreground is the former Treforest Station of the Barry Railway Company.

Pontypridd Library

Treforest Station 13th April 1968. The yellow brick edging was used on these buildings during the 1870-1900s period.

D. G. Thomas

Pontypridd Station c1853 from an engraving by Newman & Co.

Pontypridd Library

Pontypridd Station

Opened as Newbridge Station on the 8th October 1840 to goods and freight traffic, and opened on the following day for passenger services. Rebuilt and renamed as Pontypridd Station in 1891, it was further extended in 1907.

   Today there are many areas of waste ground created by the removal of disused track, with only the lines to the Rhondda valleys and Merthyr remaining. There is talk of another redesigning of this station, although British Rail spent over £113,000 modernising it in 1974.

Pontypridd Station c1891. Until its reconstruction the station consisted of two through platforms, with one 'up' and one 'down' bay. The horse was used occasionally to shunt empty railway wagons. Note wooden footbridge and the white building in the centre of the photograph which was a goods shed and office combined, Rhondda bay on right.

Pontypridd Library

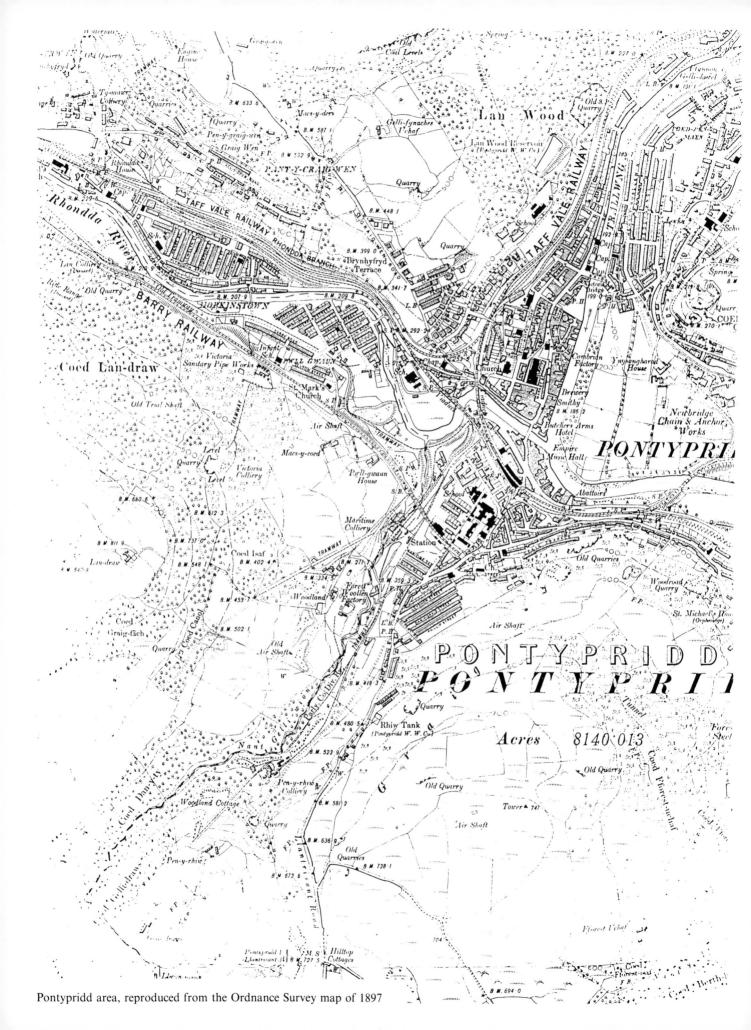

Pontypridd area, reproduced from the Ordnance Survey map of 1897

TAFF VALE RAILWAY.

R(385)
TAF

SATURDAY, DECEMBER 10th.

Northern Union International Rugby Match.

WALES v. AUSTRALIA

At PONTYPRIDD. Kick Off 2.30 p.m.

CHEAP TICKETS

WILL BE ISSUED TO

PONTYPRIDD

FROM	Times of Departure		Return Fares Third Class.	FROM	Times of Departure		Return Fares Third Class.
	A.M.	P.M.	s. d.		A.M.	P.M.	s. d.
Treherbert	11 45	12 45	2 0	Merthyr	10 25	12 45	2 3
Treorchy	11 50	12 50	2 0	Pentrebach	10 30	12 50	2 0
Ystrad	11 55	12 55	1 9	Troedyrhiw	10 35	12 55	2 0
Llwynypia	12 0	1 0	1 3	Merthyr Vale	10 40	1 0	1 6
Tonypandy	12 5	1 5	1 0	Quakers' Yard	10 45	1 5	1 0
Dinas	12 9	1 10	1 0	Aberdare	10 20	12 40	2 3
Maerdy	11 50	12 50	2 0	Aberaman	10 25	12 45	2 0
Ferndale	11 55	12 55	1 9	Mountain Ash	10 30	12 50	1 6
Ylorstown	12 0	1 0	1 3	Penrhiwceiber	10 35	12 55	1 3
	P.M.			Abercynon	10 55	1 15	1 0
Ynishir	12 5	1 10	1 0	Nelson		12 55	1 3
Porth	12 15	1 15	0 9	Cilfynydd		1 10	0 6
Trehafod	12 20	1 20	0 6	Ynysybwl	10 40	1 0	1 0
	A.M.			Penarth	11 35	12 30	3 3
Llantrisant	10 30	12 45	2 0	Penarth Dock		12 35	3 0
Cross Inn	10 35	12 50	1 3	Grangetown	11 40	—	2 9
Llantwit	10 40	1 0	1 0	Cardiff (G.W.R.)	11 50	12 50	2 6
Church Village	10 45	1 5	0 9	Cardiff (Queen St)	NOON 12 0	12 55	
	P.M.				P.M.		
Taffs Well	12 15	1 30	1 3				
Radyr	12 10	1 25	1 6	Llandaff	12 5	1 0	1 0

RETURN TRAINS will leave PONTYPRIDD as under :—

For Rhondda Branch Stations. 4.35 p.m., 5.45 p.m., 6.30 p.m., 8.0 p.m., 9a.50 p.m., 10a.20 p.m.

Ferndale 4.35 p.m., 5.45 p.m., 6.30 p.m., 8.0 p.m., 10,20 p.m.

Merthyr 4.30 p.m., 6.10 p.m., 8.20 p.m. or 10.15 p.m.

Aberdare 4.30 p.m., 5.30 p.m., 6.10 p.m., 8.20 p.m. or 10.15 p.m.

Cardiff, Penarth and intermediate Stations. 4.55 p.m., 5.25 p.m., 6.0 p.m., 6.15 p.m., 7.5 p.m., 8.10 p.m. or 9.40 p.m.

a—Except Dinas.

Children three and under twelve, half-price. No luggage allowed.
Cheap Tickets are only available to and from the Stations named upon them. Should a Ticket be used for any other Station than those named upon it, or by any other train than as specified above, it will be rendered void, and therefore the fare paid will be liable to forfeiture, and the full Ordinary fare will become chargeable. The tickets are not transferable.

The Company do not undertake that the Trains shall start or arrive at the times specified, nor will they be accountable for any loss, inconvenience or injury which may arise from delays or detention unless upon proof that such loss, inconvenience, injury, delay or detention arose in consequence of the wilful misconduct of the Company's servants.

E. A. PROSSER,

CARDIFF, November, 1921. GENERAL MANAGER.

5,000 E10402-2-8405 Western Mail Limited, Cardiff—9968D.

Courtesy Rhondda Borough Libraries

Pontypridd Station looking along platforms towards the Treforest direction. Photographed during the rebuilding in 1907, the new roof girders are already in position.

Westrail Enterprises

Pontypridd Station c1870.

Pontypridd Library

Pontypridd Station c1895, after the reconstruction of 1891, when Mr Beasley became general manager of the Taff Vale Railway Company.

Author's collection

Photographed c1904, shortly before reconstruction as one long island platform, showing the Rhondda line on the upper left and the main line to Merthyr at upper right and crossing over Brunel's viaduct.

C. W. Harris

Pontypridd Station August 1927.
R. Wilding

A photograph showing some of the work carried out to Pontypridd Station during the reconstruction of 1907. TVR engine of the 0-6-2T type, on the left.

Westrail Enterprises

Another view of Ponty-
pridd Station in 1907.
Westrail Enterprises

On the 3rd of April 1974 the secretary of
state for Wales, Mr John Morris QC MP,
decided to make a grant of £56,000 to
British Rail towards the cost of modernising Pontypridd Station. These im-
provements, costing over £113,000 included
a modern station entrance, resurfacing of
walls, a modern ticket office, and the
removal of the unnecessary canopies over
the platforms.

Pontypridd Goods Station now disused and
the land used as a car park. January 1985.
Author

The remainder of the main line stations
from Pontypridd to Merthyr Tydfil opened
in various stages. The line to Abercynon
opened in October 1840, and by 12th April
1841 this line was opened throughout to
Merthyr Taff Vale Station at Plymouth
Street. This section was ultimately doubled
throughout, by 1862 with a second viaduct
being built alongside the original Brunel
structure at Quakers Yard.

Abercynon Station
Known originally as Navigation House, but
renamed Aberdare Junction with the opening of the Aberdare branch in August 1846,
and was renamed Abercynon Station on the
1st December 1896. This station opened in
October 1840 and closed to goods traffic
on 20th April 1964.

Abercynon Station c1910. The photograph
consists of TVR 0-6-0 No. 110, and a 10 ton
coal wagon at the coaling stage. Note the
canvas rain sheet rigged over the cab of the
second engine, another 0-6-0.
Author's collection

Abercynon Station 6th May 1951.
H. C. Casserley

A general view of Abercynon Station and the engine shed, which is now used by a private firm, c1966.

B. Hamlet

Abercynon Engine Shed c1955. Also visible are the loco dept. breakdown van, tool van and mess van, a pannier tank and Class 5600 engine.

D. K. Jones

Incline Top Station

Opened in 1846 and renamed Top of the Incline Station in May 1849, this station was closed in the December of 1857. The original Abercynon to Quakers Yard section of the main line was to the left of the present day line, which contained an incline of a 1 in 22 gradient. This meant that Brunel had to install a stationary winding engine for this section, which was finally abandoned in favour of the present location of the main line in 1864.

The remains of the Top of the Incline Station after being struck by a cyclone which caused great damage to the Cilfynydd, Abercynon and Quakers Yard districts on 27th October 1913. Today the area is overgrown with trees and horses graze in the field where the station house stood.

Pontypridd Library

Close up photograph of the cyclone damage to the Top of the Incline Station, October 1913.

C. Hughes

Quakers Yard Low Level Station

Opened in 1858 and had exchange sidings with the GWR High Level Station which had opened in 1857. Today the area of the GWR station has all but gone, and a new housing estate is being built. In place of the ornate TVR station building there is now a British Rail bus shelter type structure.

Quakers Yard Low Level Station photographed on 30th November 1957.

R. M. Casserley

Merthyr Vale Station
Opened 1st June 1883, and closed for the handling of goods traffic on 25th February 1957. Still in today for passenger services but the Victorian buildings were dismantled by contractors in 1972 (as were all along this stretch of line), as they had become too expensive to be maintained by British Rail.

Merthyr Vale Station c1910
Lens of Sutton

Troed-y-Rhiw Station
Opened 12th April 1841, closed for the handling of goods traffic on 7th October 1963, still in use for passenger services.

Pentrebach Station
Opened 1st August 1886, and is still in use for passenger services.

Cartoon postcard printed in the early part of this century.
Merthyr Tydfil Public Library

Troed-y-Rhiw Station 10th August 1968.
D. G. Thomas

Pentrebach Station, showing the booking office and waiting room, c1971.
B. Morris

Brandy Bridge Junction to Mardy Junction

This section of line opened on 1st August 1877. The track and signal box were removed in 1970 and today small bushes cover most of this area. The original Taff Vale Station at Merthyr Tydfil was opened on 12th April 1841 and situated just south of the town and called Plymouth Street, renamed Merthyr Plymouth Street in July 1924.

The Vale of Neath Railway, also engineered by Brunel, made their own station at Merthyr called High Street which opened on 2nd November 1853. The approach passed over the Taff Vale line just south of Plymouth Street Station by a long viaduct. On 1st August 1877 the Taff Vale Railway and Great Western opened a joint line from Brandy Bridge to Mardy Junction. This joint line was advantageous to both companies so on the 1st August 1877 the Taff Vale Railway Company transferred its passenger services to the Merthyr High Street Station, and Plymouth Street Station was used as a goods depot. The goods depot and the junction signal box closed on 27th of November 1967 and in 1968 respectively. After closure this depot was taken over by National Carriers Limited. Today the ground is owned and used by British Telecom.

Dowlais Junction to Dowlais Iron Works Station

Opened for goods and passenger traffic on the 2nd August 1851, passengers were carried for a total of three years only, until May 1854. Although general freight was carried until 1876, mineral traffic was carried until closure of the Dowlais Iron Works in the October of 1930. The track was removed in 1945.

Merthyr High Street Station

This important station was shared by many railway companies. These included the Vale of Neath, Brecon & Merthyr, London & North Western, Great Western, Rhymney, and also the Taff Vale Railway Company.

The main line from Abercynon to Merthyr was singled in 1971.

Plymouth Street in National Carriers' days, with international traffic vans on the sidings in the middle of photograph (for shipments abroad from the nearby Hoover factory).

A. A. Smith

TRAIN LEAVING MERTHYR STATION.

Merthyr High Street Station with an LNWR train making its departure known, c1910.

Lens of Sutton

Merthyr High Street Station, frontage of booking office, 28th March 1970.

D. G. Thomas

The new building at Merthyr Station with modern-day booking office, August 1974.

British Rail

Merthyr High Street Station, goods depot in a state of dereliction, August 1985.

Branch Lines

The Rhondda Branch
Initially, only the line from Pontypridd Station to Pandy Station and the nearby colliery was used for coal traffic. This line was opened in the June of 1841, the remainder of the branch to the station at Treherbert being completed for the use of coal traffic and opened on 7th August 1856, opening for passenger services on 7th January 1863.

Gyfeillon Platform was closed in July 1918 to both passenger and goods traffic. Hafod Junction, a Barry Railway Junction with the Taff Vale Railway was opened in 1884 and was closed on 4th July 1956. Havod Station was altered to Hafod in the November of 1890 and renamed Trehafod on 1st January 1905 and was closed to the handling of goods traffic on 7th October 1963. Still in use for passenger services today.

Diesel multiple unit at Trehafod Station 13th April 1968.

D. G. Thomas

Eirw branch built to serve the nearby collieries, was a total of 73 chains in length. Eirw (or Aerw) Junction opened in 1854 and closed in October 1978.

Lewis Merthyr Collieries, Porth.

Eirw Branch showing Lewis Merthyr Collieries, Porth.

Lens of Sutton

Porth Station

The first Porth Station opened on 7th January 1863, closing on 1st July 1876, to be replaced by a new passenger station about 11 chains to the south in 1876.

The second Porth Station opened on 1st July 1876, the same day that the first one closed. Still in use for passenger services but many changes to this station have taken place. Numerous lines and sidings have been removed and the original Victorian buildings replaced with modern British Rail types. (Closed to goods traffic on 7th September 1964).

Porth Station frontage 13th April 1968.
D.G. Thomas

Porth c1900-1905, facing in the direction of Rhondda Fach Junction.

Lens of Sutton

Summer 1963 facing towards the direction of Trehafod showing Porth Station.

C.W. Harris

Pandy Station
Opened in the June of 1841, and closed entirely on 2nd August 1886, to be replaced by Dinas Station.

Pandy Station, 13th January 1879, the photograph also shows the Dinas Middle Colliery in the background with anxious colliery families awaiting news of survivors of the explosion and fire which had occurred only an hour before. (This historic photograph was rescued from a bucket containing hot ashes, by Mr C. Batstone just as it began to smoulder!)

Courtesy Mr C. Batstone

Dinas Rhondda Station c1960.

C.W. Harris

Dinas Station
Situated 10 chains west of the former Pandy Station this station was temporarily closed by the TVR on 1st of April 1917, to be reopened at a later date. Renamed by the GWR on 1st November 1927, as Dinas Rhondda Station.

The decorative footbridge was cut up in 1983, and left piled up on one of the platforms for a couple of years before eventual removal by British Rail. (Such a waste, as it would no doubt have been of use to a preservation group.)

Tonypandy and Trealaw Station
Opened on 9th March 1908, and was renamed as Tonypandy by British Rail on 7th May 1973. The station was rebuilt by British Rail as yet another bus shelter, and is still in use for passenger services.

Tonypandy Brick Yard Sidings were closed entirely by 31st January 1966.

Tonypandy and Trealaw Station facing the direction of Llywnypia c1908, the photograph would appear to have been taken some time just after the opening due to the lack of the advertising boards in evidence.

Lens of Sutton

Pwllyrhebog Goods Station
Renamed Trealaw on 1st April 1875, closed to goods traffic on 31st January 1966, this building is now used by a firm of building merchants.

Pwllyrhebog Incline
The branch of the Pwllyrhebog Incline to the Clydach Vale Colliery, from the branch junction at Tonypandy, was opened in 1863. This line was acquired by the Taff Vale Railway Company in 1896, and was closed on 1st July 1951.

The incline consisted of a 1 in 13 gradient, for a length of 1 mile, and locomotives were assisted by a counter balance rope wound round a large drum at the incline top, controlled by a powerful brake.

The summit of Pwllyrhebog Incline, 4th May 1951,

H.C. Casserley

Blaenclydach Goods Depot at the summit of the Pwllyrhebog Incline, was opened in 1863. Today there is not a great deal that can be seen of the goods yard, sidings or engine shed. Rough grass has covered most of the area and all the buildings have long since vanished, although it is still possible to walk up the incline, and in some cases one can see the lighter traces in the grass where the sleepers once lay.

Blaenclydach Engine Shed with an 0-6-0T TVR engine inside, c1949.

Real Photographs Co.

The former site of Blaenclydach Goods Depot, November 1984.

Author

Llwynypia Station
Opened in January 1863, and known originally as Llwynypia and Tonypandy Station. Renamed Llwynypia on 9th March 1908, the same day that the new passenger station (Tonypandy and Trealaw) was opened. The station was closed to the handling of goods traffic on 12th October 1964 but is still in use for passenger services.

Llwynypia Station c1900.
Rhondda Borough Libraries

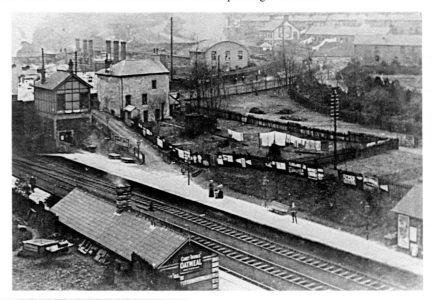

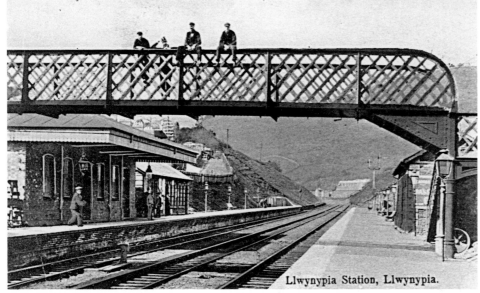

Llwynypia Station, c1910 showing the then new booking office, on the left.
Lens of Sutton

Ystrad Station with the arrival of the 5pm Treherbert train, 14th April 1902.
Rhondda Borough Libraries

Ystrad Station
Opened in 1863, and renamed Ystrad Rhondda Station in December 1930; again renamed, this time by British Rail as Ton Pentre in November 1985. (Closed to goods traffic on 3rd August 1964).

Ystrad Rhondda Station during the 1950-1955 period, facing towards Gelli.
Lens of Sutton

Gelli Platform
This was closed in November 1912 but there are some platform remains left and the footbridge gives an idea of where this halt was. All other traces have long since disappeared.

Pentre Platform
Closed in November 1912 it is believed that this halt was reopened for the embarkation of troops, during the Great War of 1914-1918, but closed shortly afterwards.

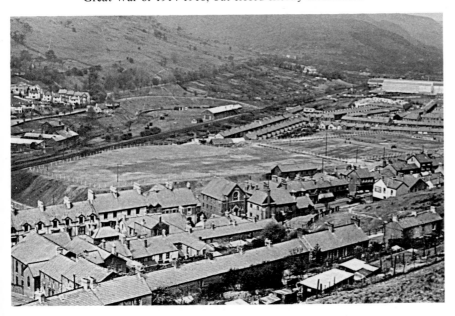

Photographed from Pleasant View above Woodfield Hotel and the Messiah Chapel, Pentre, looking across to the Pentwyn Road. The Territorial Army barracks are still used but there is no trace today of the Halt that was situated alongside, visible in the middle of the photograph.
Rhondda Borough Libraries.

Treorchy Station and Goods Depot

The Goods Depot opened in 1863, closed on 5th August 1963. Today the former goods shed is now used by a private firm as a warehouse; in fair condition but the corrugated iron sheeting is gradually rusting away. GWR pot sleepers can still be seen around the building.

Treorchy Goods Depot facing towards the station. September 1984.

Author

Treorchy Station opened in the January of 1863 and is still in use for passenger services today.

A photograph taken at the turn of century, facing towards Pentre direction, from Treorchy Station, Ocean Coal Company Wagon works are on the right, in the far background.

Westrail Enterprises

Treorchy Station, looking south east, in the early part of century.

Westrail Enterprises

Another early 20th century view of Treorchy Station. The overbridge is situated at the Treherbert end of the station, and had been heightened by over three feet from its original position.

Westrail Enterprises

A view from the same position but showing the vertical supports for the platform face now in position.

Westrail Enterprises

Treorchy Station, photographed from the 'down' booking office, looking towards Treherbert Station.

Westrail Enterprises

Steam crane working on the Taff Vale Railway, unloading timbers from open wagons for the contractors working on raising the platforms beside the 'down' booking office, facing the north west.

Westrail Enterprises

Treorchy Station, circa 1916 facing Treherbert direction.

C.W. Harris

Tylacoch Platform
Closed for passenger service in the November of 1912. Today all that remains is a grassy mound where the platform stood; a few yards up the line is the remains of the base where the signal box once stood, and a footbridge, which long ago served a purpose, but is now useless as the locals walk across the now "single" track due to lack of fencing.

Treherbert Station
Opened on 7th January 1863, closed to the handling of goods traffic on 5th August 1963, and still in use for passenger services.

Treherbert Station c1873.

C. Coles

Treherbert Station with TVR coaches in view, note the Barry Railway coach behind the station nameboard. Looking towards the Blaenrhondda direction, 27th June 1938.

H.C. Casserley

Treherbert Station, facing the direction of Treorchy, c1964.

Author's collection

Overlooking Treherbert Station and sidings, c1920.

LGRP courtesy David and Charles

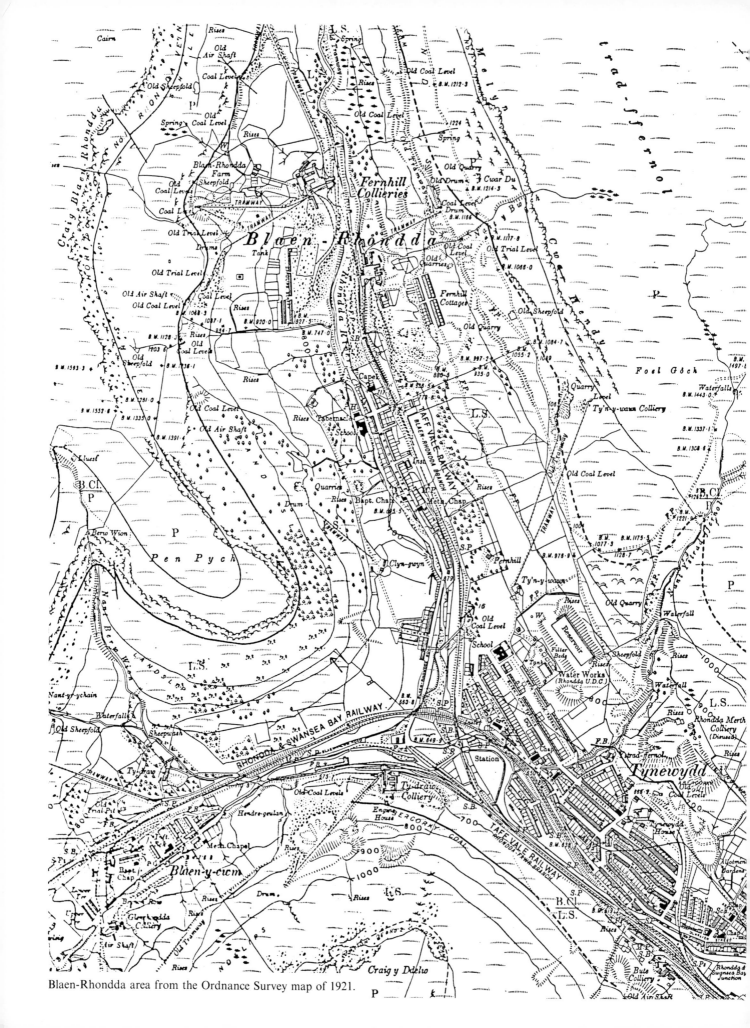

Blaen-Rhondda area from the Ordnance Survey map of 1921.

TAFF VALE RAILWAY.

DAY EXCURSION TO BRISTOL.

On MONDAY, JULY 13th, 1908.

AN EXCURSION TRAIN will be run to

BRISTOL

(Stapleton Road & Lawrence Hill Station) as under

STATIONS	Times of Departure.	Third Class Return Fares	
	a.m.	s	d
Treherbert	6 20	3	6
Treorchy	6 25		
Ystrad	6 29		
Llwynypia	6 34	3	3
Tonypandy and Trealaw	6 38		
Dinas	6 41		
Maerdy	6 15	3	6
Ferndale	6 25		
Tylorstown	6 30		
Ynyshir	6 39		
Porth	6 47		
Trehafod	6 51	3	3
Ynysybwl	7 10		
Pontypridd	7 20		
Treforest	7 25		
Taffs Well	7 35		
Radyr	7 40		
Llandaff	7 45		

Passengers from the Rhondda Branch Stations change at Pontypridd both directions.
The Return Train will leave Bristol (Lawrence Hill Station) at 8.20 p.m., and Stapleton Road at 8.25 p.m, same day.

Electric Tramway Cars run every few minutes between Stapleton Road Station and the City. Frequent Trains also run from and to Stapleton Road and Clifton Down; also Temple Meads.

Children under 3 years of age Free, 3 and under 12 Half-price. No Luggage allowed.

Should an Excursion or Cheap Ticket be used for any other Stations than those named upon it, or by any other Train than as above specified, it will be rendered void, and therefore the Fare paid will be liable to forfeiture and the Full Ordinary Fare will become Chargeable. The Tickets are not Transferable, and are only available on the day of issue.

The Issuing of Through Tickets is subject to the Conditions and Regulations referred to in the Time Tables, Books, Bills and Notices of the respective Companies and Proprietors on whose Railways they are available, and the holder, by accepting a Through Ticket agrees that the respective Companies and Proprietors are not to be liable for any loss, damage, injury, delay, or detention caused or arising off their respective Railways. The Contract and Liability of each Company and Proprietor are limited to their or his own Railway.

A. BEASLEY,
GENERAL MANAGER.

CARDIFF, June 1908. No. 5,815

Lennox Brothers, Steamship and Railway Printers, Docks, Cardiff.

Narrow gauge track used for the building of the Llynfawr Reservoir, showing the TVR North Dunraven Sidings in the background, c1908.

Rhondda Borough Libraries

Dunraven Milage Sidings, closed in 1957.

Tynewydd Milage Siding was closed entirely by 7th September 1964.

Remains of the former Taff Vale Railway, Blaenrhondda Branch, c1983. The branch is now partly built on, and more prominent in this photograph is the former Rhondda & Swansea Bay Company's line and their Blaenrhondda Station site.

Courtesy the family of the late P. Gardener

Blaenrhondda Branch Junction to the Blaenrhondda Colliery, opened in 1873. The last part of this short branch, leading to Fernhill Colliery closed in 1966.

Rhondda Fach Branch

The line from Porth to Ynishir was completed for the handling of mixed traffic by 1849 and the part from Ynishir to Ferndale was completed by the summer of 1856. Passenger services ran from Porth Station to Ferndale Station by 1876, and continued into Mardy Station in 1889. The tracks were singled on the Rhondda Fach Branch by 1965.

Porth Rhondda Fach Junction, facing towards Pontypridd, the lines on, left coming from the Rhondda Fach Branch, and those on the right coming from the Rhondda Branch, photographed in July 1921. A far different scene is presented today with only the one line going to Maerdy Colliery, which is situated at the end of this branch.

B.J. Miller

Porth Goods Station frontage, now a do-it-yourself warehouse, December 1984.
Author

Porth Goods Station closed to all traffic on 7th September 1964.

Ynishir Station c1960
Lens of Sutton

Ynishir Station closed on 15th June 1964. Today all that can be seen are the broken remains of the platforms and a council bench stands in the empty space where the booking office once was.

Wattstown Platform closed for passenger services on 12th July 1920. Today there is no visible trace left, only the road bridge and the memories of the older inhabitants.

Wattstown Goods Depot closed on 7th October 1963. This is now in private hands as a builder's merchant yard and the gate posts where the track entered the yard can still be seen, but the rest of the buildings of the depot have all gone.

Pontygwaith Halt c1910
Author's collection

Pontygwaith Halt was closed on 1st October 1914. No trace is left of this former TVR halt, only the road bridge is still there, covered in the usual graffiti.

Tylorstown Station closed for passenger services on 15th June 1964. The platforms are still in place but the only visitors are the local sheep. Tylorstown Upper and Lower Sidings closed on 7th October 1963.

Tylorstown Station and Sidings c1905, facing towards the direction of Pontygwaith area.

Lens of Sutton

Tylorstown TVR Station facing towards Ferndale.

Lens of Sutton

Ferndale Station

Opened in 1876, this station closed for passenger services on 15th June 1964, and closed to the handling of goods traffic on 7th October 1963. Today only the platforms and the retaining stone walls to prevent landslip remain. There is no trace remaining of the former engine sheds or sidings.

Cartoon style postcard, early part of the century (possibly 1900-1910).

Author's collection

Ferndale Station c1910 facing towards Tylorstown.

Lens of Sutton

Ferndale Engine Shed with GWR 0-6-2T No. 5613, 11th March 1963

D.K. Jones

Maerdy Station
Opened in June 1889, was closed for passenger services on 15th June 1964, and for the handling of goods traffic on 1st March 1956. Today most of the site of this former station is covered by the building of a private firm, but the platform is still intact. In the past the site has been regularly visited by rail tours as the sidings are still used by British Coal but closure of Maerdy Colliery and the sidings are now due soon.

Photograph showing the opening ceremony of Maerdy Station in 1889.

Lens of Sutton

GENERAL VIEW OF MARDY.

Postcard dated 14th September 1928, showing a photograph possibly taken in 1915. Note the TVR brakevan on the right.

Author's collection

Maerdy Station, 21st May 1953 with an auto train worked by GWR 2-6-2T No. 5572, waiting at the platform.
N.L. Browne

Roath Branch

Roath Branch Junction, at Mynachdy was opened in the August of 1887, but the traffic did not run until the opening of Roath Dock on 23rd April 1888. This dock covered an area of 33 acres. The Roath Branch closed on 6th May 1968. Today all that is left of this former junction and sidings are the sleepers piled up and the great areas of concrete base strewn with brambles. It is hard to believe that these sidings could once store a total of 2,240 wagons.

Taff Vale Railway 0-6-2T No. 78, on the 'down' line and laden with coal at Roath Branch Junction, 31st March 1923.

LCGB (Ken Nunn collection)

No. 375, a TVR Class A 0-6-2T with 'up' empties on the Roath Branch, 25th June 1957.

S. Rickard

Roath Power Station c1927, showing part of the Roath Branch, also the sidings and track of the TVR Roath Depot.
South Glamorgan Libraries

Roath Depot, renamed Newport Road Sidings by the GWR on 1st July 1924, closed entirely on 2nd May 1966. No trace is left today, a supermarket and car park covering the site, while most of the Roath Branch is under threat of development for housing construction.

Top:
March 20th 1940 showing the Marshalling
Sidings, Cardiff.
Associated British Ports/GWR Docks Dept.

Above
Spillers Granary, Roath Dock and Storage
Sidings, photographed in November 1957.
Associated British Ports

Right and opposite top:
Two views of the cattle lairs, Roath Dock,
photographed in May 1947. These cattle
lairs were destroyed by fire in the early part
of 1950.

Associated British Ports

A new pair of gates for the inner end of Roath Sea Lock, built by Armstrong Whitworth c1900.

Associated British Ports

Roath Basin was opened in the July of 1874, and covered an area of 12 acres. The sidings at this dock held a maximum of 1,270 wagons.

Excavation of the new Roath Dock, on 21st April 1884, facing west.

Associated British Ports

Reproduced from the Ordnance Survey map of 1901.

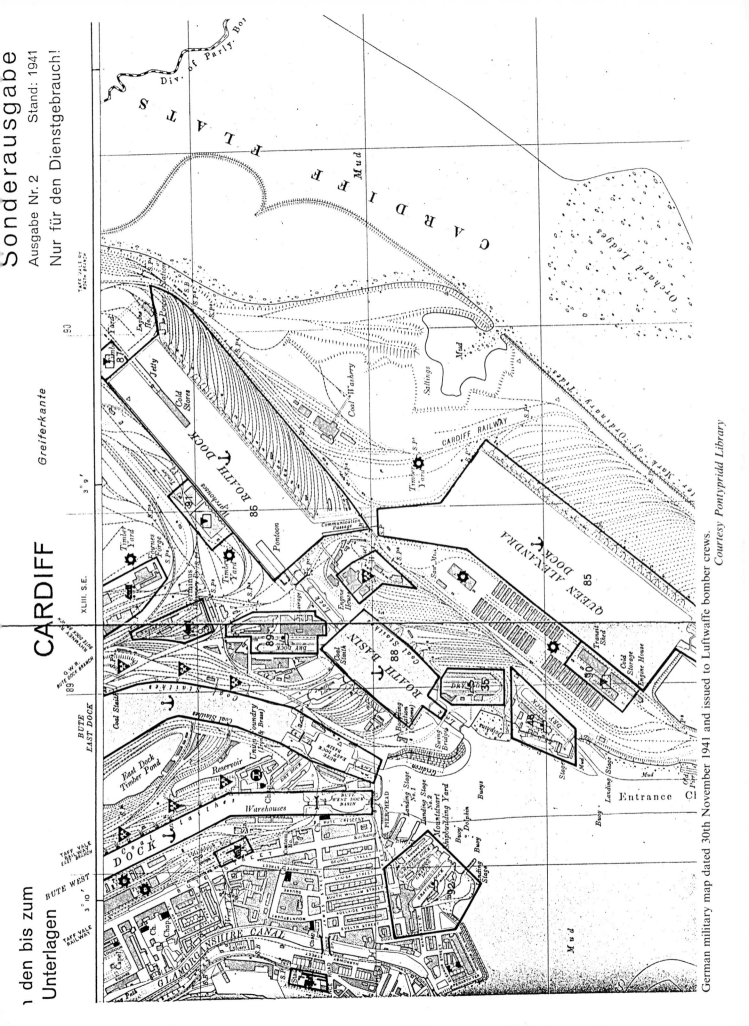

Sonderausgabe
Ausgabe Nr. 2   Stand: 1941
Nur für den Dienstgebrauch!

CARDIFF

Greiferkante

n den bis zum
Unterlagen

German military map dated 30th November 1941 and issued to Luftwaffe bomber crews.
Courtesy Pontypridd Library

Another view of the excavations of Roath Dock, taken on 21st April 1884, facing towards the north west direction.
Associated British Ports

Coal tips situated on the east side of Roath Basin, photographed at 10.45 am on 23rd April 1888, the opening day of Roath Dock.

Associated British Ports

Roath Dock photographed on the day of opening to traffic, 23rd April 1888.
Associated British Ports

Aerial view of Roath Basin and Dock, the cattle lairs are in the centre of this photograph dated c1930.

Associated British Ports

Aerial view showing Roath Basin and Dock, also plainly in view are the sidings leading to the coal tips, c1955. (A different scene compared with the Cardiff Docks of today.)

Associated British Ports

The East Branch

Bute East Dock, the first part of which was opened in the July of 1855, had a length of 1,000 feet and width of 300 feet. The work started in the early part of 1852 and once the first part of this dock was completed, the engineers, Messrs Walker, Burgess and Cooper, started work on the first part of the extension in 1855. This was completed and opened in 1857, the length then being 2,000 feet, and the width 500 feet. The final extension was started in 1857, and when this was completed, the length was 2,300 feet and width 500 feet. On the 1st September 1859 this dock was finally opened completely.

These docks were leased by the Marquis of Bute to the Taff Vale Railway, who used the coal tips on the west side of this dock, and had sidings to hold a total capacity of 872 wagons. Bute East Dock closed in 1970.

A photograph in 1980 showing the former East Junction (on the left of the dmu in the background) which took the line to the East and West Bute Docks.

D. Miller

April 22nd 1884, No. 1 coal tip, on the west side of East Dock, this photograph was taken at 3pm from aboard a vessel in dock.
Associated British Ports

April 24th 1884, showing No. 2 coal tip, which is located on the west side of East Dock. Photograph taken at 12.30pm.
Associated British Ports

July 14th 1884. Photograph taken at 10.30am, showing the coal tips No. 7 and No. 8 on the west side of Bute East Dock. Also in the picture are ships waiting for coal to be loaded.
Associated British Ports

West side of Bute East Dock, c1946, with wagons of various railway companies, including pre-Grouping; LMS, MR, GER and NER.

Associated British Ports/British Rail

BR built 2-6-2T No. 4160, waits its turn by the coaling stage at Cardiff Bute East Dock, 20th September 1963.

G. Pearce

Bute West Dock
Opened in 1839, this dock was also leased by the Marquis of Bute, to the Taff Vale Railway Company, and it was used by the TVR on the opening of the main line, on 8th August 1840. West Dock closed in 1964.

Facing north, 6th August 1930, illustration showing the TVR feeder lines to the coal hoists located on the west side of East Bute Dock, and the east side of West Bute Dock.

Associated British Ports/British Rail

Aerial view of West Bute Dock, 6th August 1930.

Associated British Ports/British Rail

Aberdare Branch
Opened completely for the handling of goods traffic on 5th August 1846, and for passenger services on 6th August 1846. Between 1840 and 1845 many collieries were opened to produce and export steam coal, all over the world. The junction at Cwmbach, serving the colliery at Abernant, opened in 1846, a total length of 49 chains. The Dare Valley line to Bwllfa Dare Colliery opened in 1866 as a private line, but it was absorbed by the Taff Vale Railway in August 1889. Both of these short branches closed in the early part of the 1960s.

The passenger services on this branch ceased on 16th March 1964, with the exception of excursion trains. The Aberdare Branch was singled in the November of 1968, with a passing loop at Abercwmboi. On the 10th August 1973 the line from Cwmbach Junction to Aberdare Low Level Station was closed and a spur from Cwmbach Junction to join the former Vale of Neath line was opened. This new spur involved the use of a bridge brought from the former Princes Risborough and Oxford branch line.

West Bute Dock, facing north, November 1944.

Associated British Ports/British Rail

A 'down' dmu at Pontcynon Halt, on 10th October 1958.

S. Rickard

Pontcynon Halt
Original name was Pontycynon Bridge Platform, the spelling being altered to read Pontcynon Bridge Platform in January 1910. Renamed Pontcynon Bridge Halt on 2nd October 1922, and finally to Pontcynon Halt on 8th June 1953. This halt was opened in the January of 1905, and was eventually closed on 16th March 1964.

Mathewstown Halt in a very dilapidated state, August 1985.

Author

Mathewstown Halt
Opened on 1st October 1914 and known originally as Mathewstown Platform. It was renamed by the GWR as Mathewstown Halt on 2nd October 1922. Closed for passenger services on 16th March 1964.

Penrhiwceiber Station
Opened on 6th August 1846 and originally known as Penrhiwceiber TVR Station. Renamed by the GWR as Penrhiwceiber Low Level Station on 1st July 1924. Closed on 16th March 1964 for passenger services, and to goods traffic on 2nd of December 1963.

Photograph taken during the early part of this century of the TVR station at Penrhiwceiber.

Lens of Sutton

Mountain Ash Oxford Street Station, TVR in June 1921.

B. J. Miller

Mountain Ash Oxford Street Station
Opened on 6th August 1846 as Mountain Ash TVR Station, renamed as Mountain Ash Oxford Street Station on 1st July 1924. The station closed on 2nd December 1963 for the handling of goods traffic, and closed on 16th March 1964 for passenger services.

Abercwmboi Platform, June 1921.

B. J. Miller

Abercwmboi Halt
Originally known as Duffryn Crossing Platform, it was renamed as Abercwmboi Platform in February 1906, and finally became Abercwmboi Halt on 2nd October 1922. This Halt was opened in January 1905, and closed for passenger services on 2nd of April 1956. Today no trace of this halt remains, only the cleared area of trees marks the place where the platform stood.

Aberaman Station looking towards the Abercwmboi direction, showing the new 'up' building, photographed at the turn of the century.

Westrail Enterprises

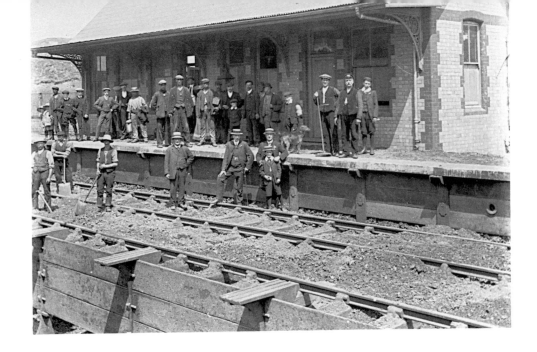

Aberaman Station, 'down' booking office, photographed at the turn of the century.

Westrail Enterprises

Treaman and Aberaman Stations

Treaman first station opened on 6th August 1846 and was closed entirely in the June of 1856. It was replaced by Treaman second station, which opened in the June of 1856 and was situated only a few chains in distance from the first.

Aberaman Station opened on 26th August 1889 and was built to replace the Treaman second station that had closed the same day, Aberaman was closed to passenger services on 16th March 1964, and to the handling of goods traffic on 2nd December 1963. In August 1985 the former site of Aberaman Station was bulldozed and levelled to become part of the route of the new trunk road to Aberdare.

Aberaman Station, showing the vertical supports, for raising the height of the 'down' side platforms c1900.

Westrail Enterprises

Aberaman Station facing towards the direction of Abercwmboi, c1910.

Lens of Sutton

An early, undated view of Aberdare TVR Station.

Cynon Valley Libraries

Aberdare Low Level Station

Opened for passenger services on 6th August 1846, known originally as Aberdare TVR Station with the suffix Low Level added by the GWR on 1st July 1924. Closed for passenger services on 16th March 1964, and to goods traffic on 3rd August 1964. The line from Pontcynon Junction to Aberdare North Junction was singled in November 1968.

Today the former TVR line at Aberdare has gone and a new trunk road has replaced it, the passenger services now run from the former GWR station at Aberdare, and then continue along the new spur at Abercwmboi, to travel along the TVR line to Abercynon.

Aberdare TVR Station facing towards Mill Street, June 1921.

B.J. Miller

Aberdare Low Level Station frontage c1966. This building was demolished in 1968 and today the station yard is used as a bus terminus.

G. Davies

Aberdare Commercial Street Platform is now completely demolished, and this site is now part of the new trunk road. The platform opened on 6th August 1846 and was closed in June 1912.

The Little Theatre and the platform of Pont Shencyn. This is just a short distance from Bwllfa Dare Junction, the Little Theatre was converted from an old train shelter, which was given by a local coal owner. It was situated at the start of the section of the TVR which ran up to the Bwllfa pits, and known as Gadlys Halt. Photograph c1950.

G. Davies

Aberdare Mill Street opened on 6th August 1846 and closed in November 1852. This halt was re-opened as Mill Street Platform in January 1905, but was also closed again in June 1912.

Bwllfa Dare Branch running from the junction with the Aberdare Branch to the Bwllfa Dare Colliery, was opened in 1886 for mineral traffic and closed entirely by 1963, with tracks lifted in 1965.

Today the Bwllfa Dare Branch is quite easy to follow, and the wooded scenery is pleasant. Also of interest are the foundations that remain of the former GWR Dare Viaduct.

The GWR Dare Viaduct, Dare Valley with a GWR train crossing above the TVR Bwllfa Dare Branch, c1880.

Cynon Valley Libraries

Taff Vale Railway Company cartoon postcard, possibly turn of the century.
Miss M. E. Loveridge

Penarth Branch

The Penarth Branch from Penarth Junction at Radyr to the Ely Tidal Harbour was opened for traffic in the August of 1859. The sidings at Radyr also opened at the same time, and lasted until their closure on 6th January 1964. The private sidings are still in use. The TVR sidings at Penarth Junction were built to hold 2,494 wagons.

Radyr Sidings, with Radyr Station on right, background. Also visible is the original TVR goods shed which was still in use, August 1985.

Author

Radyr Engine Sheds c1963.

S. Rickard

Radyr Quarry Junction opened in 1899, and in 1900 this junction linked the Llandaff Loop with the main line by crossing over the Taff River.

Ely Goods Depot
All trace of the former Ely Goods Depot has now been erased, and a school field covers this former site.

Ely Fairwater Road TVR depot, renamed Ely Goods Depot on 1st July 1924, closed 1st July 1963.

Penarth South Curve opened in the August of 1859, and the nearby Penarth North Curve sidings could hold a capacity of 134 wagons, while Sloper Road sidings held 647 wagons.

Ninian Park Halt, closed for the handling of goods traffic in April 1966. Originally known as Ninian Park Platform, used mainly for football excursion trains for the nearby Cardiff City Football Club ground.

A Class 37, passing Radyr Quarry signal box, near Llandaff Loop Junction, with a train load of coke for Barry, c1982.

A. Powell

Class 37, No. 37189, passing Ninian Park Halt 27th August 1986.

Author

Bagging coal for delivery onto road vehicles, from coal wagons, at Sloper Sidings, Virgil Street, c1964.

E. Perkins

Grangetown Station facing towards Ninian Park direction, 13th April 1968.

D. G. Thomas

Grangetown Station showing the junction to the Ferry Road line. Opened in 1859 this was the start of a short branch which led to the Ferry Road side of Ely Tidal Harbour Basin, October 1985.

Author

Llandough Platform
Closed on 1st June 1918. Today no trace of this halt remains and a poster board now marks the former site. Also, all that remains of the Llandough Sidings is a massive area of waste ground. These sidings could hold a total capacity of 978 wagons. The branch from Cogan Junction to Penarth Town Station opened for traffic on 20th February 1878.

Photograph of Cogan Junction, taken from the Barry side on 10th July 1966.

D. G. Thomas

Ely Tidal Harbour and Penarth Dock
The harbour was ready for use and opened in 1859, and Penarth Dock opened to the handling and exporting of coal traffic in 1865 with an extension opened in 1884. Penarth Dock closed in 1936, but was re-opened to handle traffic during the 1939 to 1945 war, and then remained open until 1963. When this dock finally closed to shipping the coal handling facilities had already been withdrawn the previous year.

In 1971 the former Penarth Docks were sold to Penarth Commercial Properties Limited, who have plans to transform these docks (which at one time had sidings and facilities to store 847 wagons) into a modern day marina.

Photograph showing pitching to the outside
of the sea entrance, c1865.
South Glamorgan Libraries

Penarth Dock, showing the coal drops
c1865.
South Glamorgan Libraries

View from the high ground, at the upper
end of Penarth Docks facing out to sea,
c1865.

South Glamorgan Libraries

Steam crane in use during the construction of Penarth Docks c1865.
South Glamorgan Libraries

Work in progress on the outside of the sea entrance and on the inside of the dam, Penarth Docks, c1865.
South Glamorgan Libraries

General view of the south east end of Penarth Docks in 1865.
South Glamorgan Libraries

Penarth Dock c1883
B. J. Miller collection

Taff Vale Railway Company office at
Penarth Docks 23rd August 1897.
Associated British Ports

Penarth Dock c1905.
Associated British Ports

View of the interior of the engine shed,
showing a double compound air
compressor for use during the building of
the under-water section of the subway, 1st
July 1897.

Associated British Ports

Slating the roof of the toll house, north end of the subway, which ran under the River Ely, 4th March 1898.

Associated British Ports

Group photograph of Company staff, photographed at the opening of the subway, circa 1898.

Associated British Ports

Launching of Penarth Dock Pontoon, on the 28th June 1909.

Associated British Ports

Pontoon at the Quay wall, just after the launch, 28th June 1909.

Associated British Ports

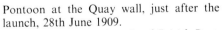

The completed pontoon in dock, with the first vessel "on board" *The Baltzig of Riga,* 8th March 1910.

Associated British Ports

Renewal of pontoon roller path. The photograph shows the lowering of the diving bell, for inspection of the path, 16th August 1920.

Associated British Ports

Penarth Docks, photographed July 1923, facing towards harbour entrance.

South Glamorgan Libraries

Penarth Docks during July 1923 facing towards Cogan Junction.

South Glamorgan Libraries

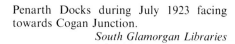

Penarth Dock with the coal drops in background, July 1923.

South Glamorgan Libraries

Penarth Dock Station
Known originally as Penarth Dock and Harbour, renamed in January 1928 as Penarth Dock Station. This station closed for passenger services on 1st January 1962. Today the former station has been converted into an armoury and shooting range!

Penarth Dock Station, c1900 from an old coloured postcard.

Author's collection

Dingle Road Halt
Opened in the April of 1904, and still in use for passenger services, this halt was rebuilt and modernised by British Rail in 1978. Known originally as Dingle Road Platform, renamed Halt on 2nd October 1922. Suffix dropped by British Rail on 5th May 1969.

Dingle Road Halt, facing towards Penarth Dock direction, January 1985.

Author

Penarth Town Station
Opened on 20th February 1878, work to extend this branch from Penarth Town Station to Biglis Junction commenced in the January of 1887. Penarth Town Station eventually closed to goods traffic on 4th April 1966.

Today part of the station is used by a private firm, and the line terminates here.

Penarth Town Station, facing Dingle Road direction, c1890.

Glamorgan Archives

GWR 0-6-2T No. 6648 at Penarth Station with the 5pm Cadoxton-Cardiff train, 24th March 1962.

G. Pearce

The Cadoxton Branch

The Cadoxton Branch from Penarth Town Station to Biglis Junction commenced in the January of 1887, the first part of this branch from Penarth Town to Lavernock, opened on 1st December 1887. The remainder – to Biglis Junction – opened on 20th December 1888. The branch closed on 7th October 1968 to goods traffic, and on 6th of May 1968 for passenger services.

No. 3729 0-6-0PT on the 10.20am Grangetown-Sully freight, passing Penarth Town Station, in 1953.

S. Rickard

Penarth-Cadoxton 1.10pm at Alberta Place Halt, with the train setting down four passengers 16th November 1967.

D. G. Thomas

Alberta Place
Opened October 1904, renamed Alberta Place Halt on 1st October 1923, closed for passengers on 6th May 1963.

Lower Penarth Halt, facing Alberta Place direction, date unknown.

Lens of Sutton

Lower Penarth Halt
Opened on 1st December 1888, known originally as Lower Penarth, renamed Lower Penarth Halt on 30th September 1935. Closed for passenger services on 14th June 1954.

Contractor's engine on the TVR Cadoxton Branch at Lavernock Cutting prior to the opening of the branch, c1887.

South Glamorgan Libraries

TVR occupational bridge, which was built in eleven days, situated at Lower Penarth, c1887.

South Glamorgan Libraries

Lavernock Halt was opened on 1st December 1887, and closed on 6th May 1968. Today this site is privately owned, the platforms are still visible and also, a few yards in the distance, can be seen the former goods shed. This is also now owned by a private firm and has been well maintained and preserved. Closed to goods traffic on 7th October 1963.

Lavernock Halt 15th August 1966.
D. G. Thomas

Swanbridge Halt 4th April 1969.
D. G. Thomas

Swanbridge Halt
Opened on 20th December 1888, and closed on 6th May 1968. Today all that remains of Swanbridge is the railbridge and some wooden sleepers. Most of the former site is covered with brambles and wild flowers, the ballast is still visible amongst the patches of grass.

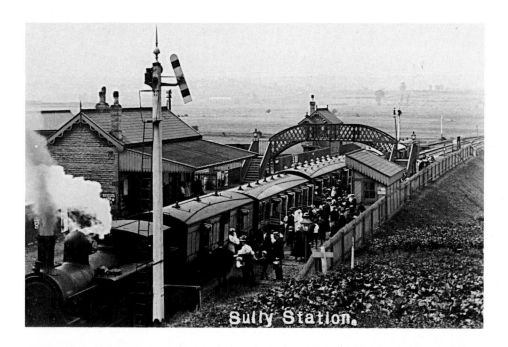

Sully Station c1912.
Welsh Folk Museum, St Fagans

Sully Station
Opened on 20th December 1888, closed to goods traffic on 7th October 1963, and for passenger services on 6th May 1968. Today nothing remains of Sully Station and the former site is now a telephone exchange.

No. 4123 2-6-2T on a Cardiff General train, at Sully Station, 23rd March 1957.

S. Rickard

A contractor's engine on top of Biglis Bridge, which was situated at the junction of the Barry and Sully road, possibly on bridge testing trials, as it was photographed just prior to the opening of the branch, circa 1888. This bridge was demolished in 1973.

South Glamorgan Libraries

Biglis Goods Depot and Sidings
Closed to the handling of goods traffic, on 1st April 1925. Today there is no trace left, only a muddy stretch of land where the track, sidings and the buildings once were. This part of the Cadoxton Branch now belongs to a tyre company.

Cadoxton Station TVR Siding
Taff Vale Railway trains ran from Penarth to Cadoxton Station using the TVR siding there, via Biglis Junction. These sidings were extended on 20th December 1888 for the handling of goods traffic, and in the August of 1889 for passenger services.

The name Cadoxton was used from 1st December 1896, as it was previously known as Biglis Station.

The TVR were given running powers to Cadoxton Station in 1888, but the Barry Railway would not allow TVR trains into Cadoxton. The case was taken before the Railway and Canal Commission and the Taff Vale Railway entered Cadoxton in 1890. Today much of the platforms and the steps leading from the TVR platform, going under the main line, can still be seen, although brambles are gradually creeping onto this now disused area.

No. 6648 0-6-2T, at Cadoxton, with the 5pm train to Cardiff General Station, on 24th March 1962. The TVR Platform steps can be seen just to the left of the locomotive.

G. Pearce

HALF-HOLIDAY EXCURSIONS

TO SEA-SIDE AND COUNTRY.

RETURN TICKETS at reduced fares are issued between the undermentioned Stations to enable passengers to take short trips into the Country.

Day	From	To	First Class s. d.	Second Class s. d.	Third Class s. d.
Wednesdays and Saturdays, also on Monday May 27th and Tuesday May 28th. No bookings on May 27th and 28th	CARDIFF (Queen St.) Do. Do. Do. Do. Do. Do.	Llandaff Radyr Taffs Well Penarth Lower Penarth Lavernock, Swanbridge, or Sully Cadoxton (T.V.)			
	Do. Do.	Penarth Lower Penarth Lavernock, Swanbridge, or Sully Cadoxton (T.V.)			
	CARDIFF G.W. & R'side Do. Do. Do.	Penarth Lower Penarth Lavernock, Swanbridge, or Sully Cadoxton (T.V.)			
	GRANGETOWN Do. Do. Do.	Lower Penarth Lavernock, Swanbridge, or Sully Cadoxton (T.V.) Nelson			
Thurs. & Sats.	PONTYPRIDD				
Thursdays, Saturdays, Sundays, and also on Monday May 27th & Tuesday May 28th.	Porth Trehafod Pontypridd Treforest Taffs Well Radyr Llandaff	Penarth Do. Do. Do. Do. Do. Do.			

These Tickets will be available on the forward journey by any train after 11.30 a.m., and are available to return by any ordinary train after 4.0 p.m. on the day of issue.

Passengers from these stations may break their outward or return journey at Cardiff.

Places of interest and other attractions in the vicinity of the Stations named.

LLANDAFF.—The Cathedral, Boating on the River Taff, and Country walks.

RADYR.—Golf Links.

TAFFS WELL.—Castell Cock, "Garth Mountain," the Potteries, Nantgarw, and the famous Mineral Bath.

LAVERNOCK AND SULLY.—Splendid Sea View, and very pleasant rambles along the Cliffs between those places and in the neighbourhood.

PENARTH.—Extensive beach, esplanade and pier, and a beautiful sea view. On the esplanade are magnificent public salt and fresh water baths. The Flat and Steep Holmes and the Somersetshire coast can be seen from the beach and cliffs, as well as the shipping passing up and down the Bristol Channel. From the north-eastern side of Penarth Head there is a splendid view of Cardiff and the Docks. The Windsor Gardens extend along the cliffs (admission by season or day ticket), and afford a most enjoyable promenade, during the summer a band plays in the grounds occasionally. Delightful walks may be taken along the cliffs towards Lavernock, Sully, and Barry and in other directions, amidst scenery of a varied and charming description. Boating and Bathing when the tide serves.

33

MARKET TICKETS.

MARKET TICKETS are issued as under. They are only available by the trains named and on the day of issue, if used otherwise the ordinary fares will be charged.

Each holder of a Market Ticket is allowed to carry a basket or package not exceeding 60lbs. in weight free; all goods in excess of this weight must be paid for at the rate of 1s. 2d. per cwt.

To	From	3rd Class return fare	Market Days	Trains — Forward Journey	Trains — Return Journey
Cardiff	Cross Inn	1 7	Saturdays	a.m. 10 39 / p.m. 12 54	3 35 p.m. 7 55 p.m. 9.15 p.m.
"	Llantwit	1 5	"	10 46 / 1 1	
"	Church Village	1 3	"	10 49 / 1 ...	
"	Pontypridd	1 2	"	9 ... / 1 20	
"	Treforest	1 0	"	9 13 / 1 21	
"	Taffs Well	0 6	"	9 22 / 1 33	
"	Radyr	0 6	"	9 27 / 1 38	
"	Llandaff (for Whitchurch)	0 5	"	9 33 / 1 44	
Pontypridd	Cowbridge	1 6	Wednesdays and Saturdays	a.m. 7 20 / p.m. 5 5	11 20 a.m. 2 0 p.m. 4 20 p.m. 6 35 p.m. also on Saturdays at 9 50 p.m.
"	Ystradowen	1 4	"	7 26 / 5 13	
"	Llanharry	1 1	"	7 32 / 5 19	
"	Llantrisant	0 9	"	7 42 / 5 25	
"	Cross Inn	0 7	"	7 50 / 5 35	
"	Church Village	0 6	"	8 1 / 5 42 / 5 46	
"	Treherbert	1 2	"	a.m. 7 40 / 10 10 / p.m. 3 25 4 20	11 18 a.m. 1 40 p.m. 3 18 p.m. 5 10 p.m. 5 47 p.m. also on Saturdays at 11 3 p.m.
"	Treorchy	1 0	"	7 45 / 10 15 / 3 30 4 25	
"	Ystrad	0 10	"	7 50 / 10 20 / 3 35 4 29	
"	Llwynypia	0 9	"	7 55 / 10 25 / 3 40 4 34	
"	Dinas	0 7	"	8 0 / 10 30 / 3 45 4 39	
"	Porth	0 5	"	8 7 / 10 36 / 3 52 4 45	
"	Maerdy	1 0	"	7 40 / 10 20 / 3 25	11 18 a.m. 1 40 p.m. 4 10 p.m. 6 30 p.m.
"	Ferndale	0 10	"	7 46 / 10 26 / 3 31	
"	Tylorstown	0 8	"	7 52 / 10 32 / 3 37	
"	Ynyshir	0 6	"	7 57 / 10 37 / 3 42	
"	Mountain Ash	0 10	"	8 0 / 10 40 / 3 40	
"	Penrhiwceiber	0 8	"	8 4 / 10 44 / 3 44	
"	Quakers Yard	0 7	"	8 8 / 10 55 / 2 52	
"	Ynysybwl	0 6	"	7 55 / 10 40 / 2 35	
"	Abercynon	0 5	"	8 17 / 11 4 / 3 1 1 53	
"	Nelson	0 9	"	7 52 / 10 45 / 3 30	11 20 a.m. 1 55 p.m. 6 38 p.m. 8 52 also on Saturdays at 8 30 p.m.
Cowbridge	Pontypridd	1 6	Tuesdays	8 33 a.m. / 11 20 a.m.	2 48 p.m. 5 5 p.m.
"	Treforest	1 5	"	8 37 / 11 24	
"	Church Village	1 3	"	8 45 / 11 32	
"	Llantwit	0 10	"	8 48 / 11 35	
"	Cross Inn	0 10	"	8 54 / 11 41	
"	Llanharry	0 6	"	9 5 / 12 6 p.m.	
"	Llantrisant	0 4	"	9 15 / 12 9	
"	Ystradowen	0 4	"	9 55 / 12 15	
"	Aberthaw	0 7	"	10 4 / 2 20	
"	St. Athan Rd.		"	/ 2 31	
"	St. Mary Church Rd.	0 3	"		
Merthyr	Abercynon	1 0	Fridays	8 32 a.m. / 9 42 a.m.	2 30 and 4 22 p.m.
"	Quakers Yard	0 7	"	8 40 / 9 50	
"	Merthyr Vale	0 7	"	8 46 / 9 56	
"	Troedyrhiw	0 5	"	8 51 / 10 1	
Merthyr	Abercynon	1 0	Saturdays	11 24 a.m. / 4 5 p.m.	4 22 p.m. 5 40 p.m. 7 20 p.m. 9 5 p.m. and 10 30 p.m.
"	Quakers Yard	0 9	"	11 32 / 4 17	
"	Merthyr Vale	0 7	"	11 38 / 4 21	
"	Troedyrhiw	0 5	"	11 43 / 4 28	
Aberdare	Abercynon	0 10	Saturdays	11 30 a.m. 3 28 p.m. 4 22 p.m.	4 22 p.m. 5 45 p.m. 7 20 p.m. and 9 5 p.m.
"	Penrhiwceiber	0 7	"	11 38 3 36 4 30	
"	Mountain Ash	0 5	"	11 42 3 40 4 34	
"	Aberaman	0 3	"	11 45 3 47 4 41	

TRAINS AND RAIL MOTOR CARS (Sundays excepted) BETWEEN
MAINDY (North Road),
CATHAYS (Woodville Road Bridge) & CARDIFF (Queen Street and Docks)

Fares -
{ Between Maindy, Cathays, and Cardiff (Queen Street), 1d.
Between Cardiff (Queen Street) and Cardiff Docks, 1d.
Between Maindy, Cathays, and Cardiff Docks, 2d.

Weekly Workmen's Tickets are Issued between Cathays (Woodville Road) and Cardiff Docks at a fare of One Shilling. These Tickets may be obtained at Cardiff Docks Station on Saturdays for the ensuing week.

DOWN.

Cathays W'dville Road dep.	Maindy North Road dep.	Cardiff Queen Street dep.	Cardiff Docks arr.		
A.M.	A.M.	A.M.	A.M.		
...	...	5§46	5§50	...	...
5§47	...	5§52	5§56	...	...
...	...	7·31	7·35	...	...
8 28	8 31	8 35	8 39	...	...
...	...	8·39	8·43	...	...
...	...	8·48	8·52	...	...
8 48	8 51	...	8 58	...	...
...	...	9· 3	9· 7	...	...
...	...	x9 10	9 11	...	...
9 7	9 10	...	9 17	...	...
...	...	x9·28	9·33	...	...
...	...	9·39	9·43	...	...
9 34	9 39	9 43	9 47	...	...
9 50	10 4	10 8	10 12	...	...
...	...	10 45	10 49	...	...
...	...	11·36	11·40	...	...
11 55	...	11 59	12 3	...	...
P.M.	...	P.M.	P.M.		
12 23	P.M.	12 27	12 31	...	...
12 47	12 50	12 55	12 59	...	...
1 16	1 13	1 17	1 21	...	...
1s43	1s45	1s52	1s56	...	...
...	...	xs2· 2	s2· 6	...	...
2 6	2 9	...	2 16	...	...
...	...	2·20	2·24	...	...
2 25	2 28	2 32	2 36	...	...
...	...	2 4	2 52	...	...
...	...	x3 30	3 34	...	...
...	...	xs3 55	3s59	...	...
...	...	4x18	4x23	...	...
...	...	...	...	...	...
5s10	5s14	5s19	5s23	...	...
5s32	5s36	5s41	5s45	...	...
...	...	6 3	6 7	...	...
...	...	6·43	6·47	...	...
...	...	7·38	7·42	...	...

UP.

Cardiff Docks dep.	Cardiff Queen Street dep.	Cathays W'dville Road arr.	Maindy North Road arr.		
A.M.	A.M.	A.M.	A.M.		
6 0	6 4	...	...		
6·20	6·24	...	...		
7 10	7 14	...	...		
8 40	8 44	8 47	8 50		
9 0	9 4	9 6	9 9		
9 20	9 29	9 33	9 36		
9 50	9 55	9 58	10 1		
10·10	10·14	...	...		
10 35	10 39	...	...		
...	10 59	11 1	11 4		
11 0	11 4	11 6	...		
P.M.	P.M.	P.M.	P.M.		
12 20	12 25	12 28	12 30		
12 40	12 44	12 46	12 49		
12·52‡	12s56*	...	...		
1 2	...	1 0	1 12		
1* 54	11 0*	...	...		
1s30	1s35	1s37	1s44		
1·30z	1·35z	1·38z	1·11z		
1 58	2 3	2 5	2 8		
2 18	2 23	2 24	2 27		
2 48	2 53	...	...		
3 5	3 9	...	...		
3 40	3 44	...	...		
4s12	4s16	...	...		
4 25	4 30	4 33	4 36		
5s 3	...	5s 9	5s13		
5·47	6*·111	...	...		
5s25	...	5s31	5s34		
5·30	5·34	...	...		
5s47	...	5s53	5s56		
5·53	5·56	...	...		
6s11	6s16	6s19	6s22		
6 35	6 40	6 43	6 46		
7·25	7·29	...	...		
8 49	8 54	8 54	...		
10 25	10 28	10 31	...		

*Denotes train. Trips not so marked are run by Cars. † Conveys Workmen as well as Ordinary Passengers on Sats.
‡ Conveys Workmen as well as Ordinary Passengers except on Sats. when Ordinary Passengers only will be conveyed. s Not run on Saturdays.
§ A Carriage for Workmen is attached to this Car except on Bank Holidays.
x All Down Trains and Cars for Cardiff Docks leave Cardiff (Queen St.) from the Down Platform, except those marked x, which leave from the Up Platform. z Saturdays only, and conveys Workmen as well as Ordinary Passengers.
Workmen in dirty clothes will not be permitted to ride in the Cars.
Smoking is prohibited in the Cars except where special compartments are provided for the purpose.
The accommodation for Luggage on the Cars being limited, the Company do not bind themselves to convey by the Cars other than hand luggage at the Passenger's own risk.
Single Journey Third Class Tickets only will be issued for use on the Cars, but Season Tickets will be available by the Cars between Maindy (North Road) and Cathays (Woodville Road), Queen Street and Cardiff Docks.
Horses, corpses, carriages, and other traffic requiring a special vehicle will not be conveyed by the Cars.

For particulars of Saturday to Monday Bookings see page 70

TRAINS AND STEAM MOTOR CARS.
Aberthaw, Cowbridge, Llantrisant and Pontypridd.

UP.

			A.M.	A.M.	A.M.	A.M.	A.M.	A.M.	P.M.	P.M.	P.M.	P.M.	P.M.	P.M.	P.M.	
			...	...	Car	...	Car	...	...	Car	...	...	Car	...	Car	...
Aberthaw	...	dep	...	...	7 55	...	11 35	...	...	4 37	...	...	...	...	8 13	...
St. Athan Road	...	,,	...	...	7 56	...	11 38	...	...	4 40	...	...	...	...	8 16	...
Llanbethery Platform	,,	...	...	7 59	...	11 41	...	...	4 43	...	...	...	...	8 19	...	
St. Mary Church Road	,,	...	...	8 5	...	11·47	...	...	4 49	...	...	...	...	8 25	...	
St. Hilary Platform	,,	...	...	8 8	...	11 50	...	...	4 52	...	...	...	...	8 28	...	
Cowbridge	...	arr	Car	...	8 13	Car	11 55	Car	Car	4 57	...	...	Car	...	8 33	...
Cowbridge	...	dep	6 55	...	8 16	10 0	12 0	1 38	2 55	5 0	...	6 40	8 38			
Aberthin Platform	,,	6 58	...	8 19	10 3	12 3	1 41	2 58	5 3	...	6 43	8 41				
Trerhyngyll & Maendy	,,	7 0	...	8 21	10 5	12 5	1 43	3 0	5 5	...	6 45	8 43				
Ystradowen	,,	7 5	...	8 26	10 10	12 10	1 48	3 5	5 10	...	6 50	8 48				
Llanharry	,,	7 10	...	8 31	10 15	12 15	1 53	3 10	5 15	...	6 55	8 53				
Llantrisant, G.W.R.	arr	7 14	...	8 35	10 19	12 19	1 57	3 14	5 19	...	6 59	8 57				
Llantrisant, G.W.R.	dep	8 22	...	9 17	10 24	12 57	2 6	3 26	5 35	...	7 35	9 52				
Cardiff G.W.R.	arr	8 52	...	9 42	10 47	1 15	2 32	3 53	6 1	...	8 5	10 9				
Llantrisant G.W.R.	dep	7 20	Car	8 40	10 30	12 50	2 18	3 40	5 23	6 37	7 15	9 7				
Cross Inn for Llantris't	,,	7 28	8 10	8 47	10 37	12 57	2 25	3 48	5 30	6 15	7 22	9 7				
Beddau Platform	,,	7 31	8 15	8 52	10 42	1 2	2 30	3 53	5 35	6 20	7 27	9 12				
Llantwit	,,	7 37	8 23	8 59	10 46	1 6	2 34	3 58	5 42	6 24	7 31	9 16				
Church Village	,,	7 40	8 26	9 2	10 49	1 9	2 37	4 1	5 45	6 27	7 34	9 19				
Tonteg Platform	,,	7 44	8 30	9 6	10 53	1 13	2 41	4 5	5 49	6 31	7 38	9 23				
Treforest	,,	7 49	8 35	9 11	10 58	1 18	2 46	4 11	5 55	6 37	7 44	9 29				
Pontypridd Junction	arr	7 52	8 38	9 14	11 1	1 21	2 49	4 14	5 58	6 40	7 47	9 32				
Connecting trains leave Pontypridd for—																
Aberdare	...	at	8 12	...	9 33	11 23	1 47	3 32	4 27	6 12	...	8 18	10 12			
Rhondda Branches	,,	8 35	8 55	9 49	11 23	1 33	3 6	4 32	6 30	...	8 8	9 48				
Merthyr	...	,,	8 20	...	9 33	11 18	1 47	3 32	4 27	6 12	...	8 18	10 12			
Cardiff	...	,,	8 18	9 0	9 54	11 13	1 21	A	4 29	6 9	7 3	8 12	9 44			

DOWN.

Connecting trains arr. Pontypridd from—			A.M.	A.M.	A.M.	A.M.	P.M.	P.M	P.M.	P.M.	P.M.	P.M.	P.M.	
			Car	Car	Car	Car	Car	Car			Car	Car	Car	Car
Cardiff	...	at	6 59	8 15	9 44	11 10	1 42	2 37	4 24	5 6	6 27	8 15	10 9
Merthyr	,,	8 25	9 6	11 15	12 62	4 26	...	6 24	2	9 41			
Rhondda	,,	6 57	8 15	9 50	11 10	4 12	4 51	4 4	5 56	7 8	8 10	9 40
Aberdare	,,	...	8 25	9 46	11 4	1 26	2 46	4 26	5 15	6 24	8 2	9 41
Pontypridd Junction	dep	7 5	8 36	10 0	11 28	1 49	3 12	4 35	5 26	6 38	8 18	10 15
Treforest	,,	7 9	8 40	10 4	11 32	1 53	3 16	4 37	5 24	6 42	8 22	10 19
Tonteg Platform	,,	7 16	8 47	10 11	11 39	2 0	3 23	4 44	5 31	6 49	8 29	10 26
Church Village	,,	7 20	8 51	10 15	11 43	2 4	3 27	4 48	5 35	6 53	8 34	10 30
Llantwit	,,	7 23	8 56	10 18	11 46	2 7	3 30	4 51	5 40	6 56	8 37	10 33
Beddau Platform	,,	7 27	9 0	10 22	11 51	2 12	3 34	4 55	5 47	0 0	8 41	10 37
Cross Inn for Llantris't	,,	7 33	9 5	10 27	11 55	2 16	3 38	4 59	5 48	7 5	8 46	10 41
Llantrisant, G.W.R.	arr	...	9 10	10 33	12 0	2 21	3 43	5 4	5 53	7 10	8 51	10 46
Cardiff G.W.R.	dep	...	7 39	9 57	11 50	1 55	2 40	...	5 16	6 50	...	9B10
Llantrisant, G.W.R.	arr	...	8 10	10 27	12 20	2 20	3 1	...	5 44	7 13	...	10B10
Llantrisant, G.W.R.	dep	9 15	10 38	12 27	2 24	3 48	...	5 58	7 30	9 10	10 51	
Llanharry	,,	9 21	10 44	12 33	2 30	3 54	...	6 27	7 36	9 16	10 57	
Ystradowen	,,	9 26	10 49	12 38	2 35	3 59	...	6 7	7 41	9 21	11 2	
Trerhyngyll & Maendy	,,	9 29	10 52	12 41	2 38	4 2	...	6 10	7 44	9 17	11 5	
Aberthin Platform	,,	Car	9 31	10 54	12 43	2 40	4 4	...	6 12	7 46	9 19	11 7
Cowbridge	,,	arr	9 34	10 57	12 46	2 43	4 7	...	6 15	7 49	9 22	11 10
Cowbridge	...	dep	7 30	...	11 0	...	...	4 9	...	...	7 52	...	...
St. Hilary Platform	,,	7 35	...	11 6	...	...	4 16	...	...	7 57	...	...	
St. Mary Church Road	,,	7 38	...	11 9	...	...	4 19	...	...	8 0	...	...	
Llanbethery Platform	,,	7 44	...	11 15	...	...	4 25	...	...	8 6	...	...	
St. Athan Road	,,	7 47	...	11 18	...	...	4 28	...	...	8 9	...	...	
Aberthaw	,,	7 49	...	11 20	...	...	4 30	...	...	8 11	...	...	

Horses, corpses, carriages and other traffic requiring a special vehicle will not be conveyed by the Cars.
No Sunday Service.   A A connecting train for Cardiff leaves Treforest at 2.53 p.m.
B On Saturdays Cardiff dep. 9.53 p.m., Llantrisant arrive 10.20 p.m.

For particulars of Saturday to Monday Bookings see page 79.

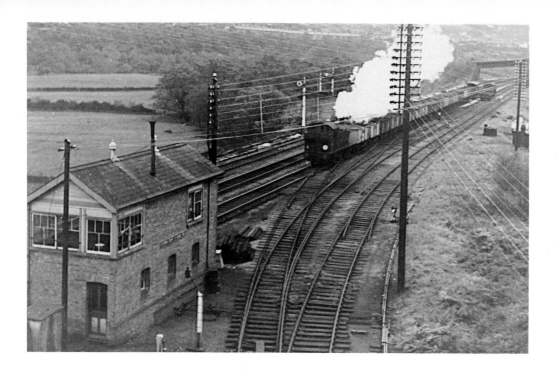

No. 5644 0-6-2T with 'up' freight at Clydach Court Junction, 5th November 1958.

S. Rickard

Ynysybwl Branch

The Ynysybwl Branch opened for the handling of goods and coal traffic from Lady Windsor Colliery in 1886, (via Ynysybwl Junction which is near Stormstown Sidings) to Abercynon Station. Passenger services started in March 1890.

The passenger services between Pontypridd Station and Ynysybwl started on 1st November 1904, via Clydach Court Junction. Originally passenger services were to Abercynon only, but once the new junction at Clydach Court was opened passenger trains (as well as goods) could travel to Pontypridd. The Ynysybwl Branch closed for passenger services on 28th July 1952, and to the handling of goods traffic on 2nd November 1959. It is still in use for the coal traffic from Lady Windsor Colliery.

Clydach Court Halt was opened in the July of 1917 as Clydach Court Platform; renamed by the GWR on 2nd October 1922, as Clydach Court Halt and closed on 28th July 1952. Today the halt has gone, the site lying buried under the new road to Ynysybwl village.

Ynysybwl South Curve was opened in 1900, joining Clydach Court Junction to the Clydach Loop Junction, eventually closing on 28th July 1952.

Ynysybwl New Road Platform, opened on 1st November 1904, and closed on 12th September 1932. Reopened and renamed Halt by the GWR on 7th May 1945. Closed to passengers on 28th July 1952.

Ynysybwl New Road Halt, facing towards Ynysybwl village direction, January 1985.

Author

Robertstown Halt, date unknown.

BR/Railprint

Robertstown Halt
Opened on 1st November 1904 as Robertstown Platform, this was renamed Robertstown Halt on 2nd October 1922. Closed for passenger services on 28th July 1952. Today all that is left is the platform, which is now used as the base for some private garages. The trackbed can be followed easily, although most of it has been split up into private holdings as it winds its way through the village of Ynysybwl.

Ynysybwl Station c1900.

Author's collection

Ynysybwl Station
Opened for the handling of goods traffic in 1886, and for passenger services in 1890. Eventually this station closed for goods traffic November 1959, and to passenger services on 28th July 1952. Today the buildings are still in very good condition, and are owned by a private bus company, but the tracks have long since been lifted.

A SLS special tour at Ynysybwl Station, facing towards Pontypridd direction, 11th July 1959.

S. Rickard

Old Ynysybwl Halt
Opened on 17th October 1904 as Old Ynysybwl Platform, this halt was renamed by the GWR as Old Ynysybwl Halt on 2nd October 1922. It closed to the handling of coal traffic on 22nd September 1949 when the Mynachty Colliery closed. Closed for passenger services on 28th July 1952 and finally to the handling of all goods traffic in November 1959. Today this halt can still be seen, and the trackbed is easily traced, although waterlogged in places.

No. 6411 an 0-6-0PT at Old Ynysybwl Halt, 11th September 1951.

H. C. Casserley

Old Warehouse Siding

This former TVR siding can still be seen, and the platform is still sound, the buildings have all gone but the foundations are still there half hidden amongst the trees and undergrowth of the forest. The remains of this former TVR line to the collieries can still be followed, alongside the river, past the picnic area for almost a half a mile further on, before disappearing.

Llancaiach Branch

Pont Shon Norton Junction to the Cilfynydd Albion Colliery, opened for the handling of goods and coal in 1887. This line was eventually extended to join the old Llancaiach Branch at Ynysdwr Junction. The original branch, which ran from Stormstown Junction via Stormstown Viaduct to Nelson Station, was opened in 1841.

The branch from Pont Shon Norton to Nelson Station, via Cilfynydd was opened for passenger services on 1st June 1900 and was closed entirely on 12th September 1932.

Photograph of the first Berw Road Platform, c1905.

Author's collection

Today, no trace is left of either Pont Shon Norton Junction, or this first Berw Road Halt, although the line of the former TVR branch can still be seen. It is now gradually becoming overgrown.

The Second Berw Road Halt, c1969, facing towards Pont Shon Norton Junction.

B. Morris

Berw Road Halt
The first Berw Road Platform, opened for passenger services on 17th October 1904, was temporarily closed on 1st July 1906. The platform was moved and re-opened sometime during July 1908. Renamed Berw Road Halt on 2nd October 1922 it eventually closed on 12th September 1932. Today the only trace of this former halt is the iron gate of TVR design, which is still in place at the entrance under Berw Road Bridge.

Photograph showing the cast iron platform frontage of the second Berw Road Halt, stamped "E D" and "TVR", 1967.

C. W. Harris

Coed Pen Maen Station
Opened for passenger services on 1st May 1905, it temporarily closed on 1st June 1915 and was re-opened at a later date, finally closing on 12th of September 1932. Today no trace of this former TVR station can be found, although it is still possible to follow the line and the area where the station stood is littered with rubbish.

Remains of the site of the former Cilfynydd Station, with Albion Colliery in the background. Photographed on 2nd March 1968.

J. Morgan

Cilfynydd Station opened for passenger services on 1st June 1900, this service ceased on 12th September 1932 and the station was closed entirely by the end of 1949. Today the A470 trunk road has been built over the site of this former TVR station.

Traveller's Rest Station was opened for passenger services on the 1st May 1901. Known as Abercynon Upper it was renamed as Traveller's Rest by the GWR on 1st July 1924. Closed for passenger services on 12th September 1932. This station site has also been buried under tons of earth by the side of the A470 trunk road.

Llanfabon Road Platform opened for passenger services on 1st November 1904 and was renamed Llanfabon Halt on 2nd October 1922. Closure took place on 12th September 1932. All that remains today of this halt are a few mounds of earth.

Nelson TVR Station, c1920.

R. Phillips

Nelson Station
Opened in June 1900, and renamed by the GWR as Nelson "Glam" Station, so as not to cause confusion with the Nelson Station in Monmouthshire. but renamed again, back to Nelson, on 1st July 1924. This station closed for passenger services on 12th September 1932, and closed to the handling of goods traffic by the end of 1939. The station site now lies buried beneath the bus depot at Nelson village, the only remains left being the road bridge.

Llantrisant Branch
This branch, running between Llantrisant Junction and Maesaraul Junction, was open to goods traffic on 1st December 1863, and for passenger services on 21st January 1875. The branch closed for passenger services on 31st March 1952 and to goods traffic on 7th September 1963.

Tonteg TVR Halt
Opened in May 1905 as Tonteg Platform, renamed as Halt on 1st October 1923 and closed on 5th May 1930. Today this former halt is covered with trees and only the rail bridge remains to remind us of the track that once was there. When the original TVR Llantrisant Branch was closed a new GWR junction with the former Barry Railway line at Tonteg Junction was opened on 10th July 1930, to connect with the main line at Treforest Junction, near Pontypridd. This ex Barry junction closed on 31st March 1952.

Collett GWR 0-6-2T No. 5641 passing Tonteg on the 2.04pm ex Treforest-Cwm Colliery freight, on 7th April 1964.

D. G. Thomas

Church Village Station was opened in the January of 1875 and renamed Church Village Halt on 14th March 1932. It was renamed as Church Village Station at a later date, closing for passenger services on 31st March 1952. This former station is now privately owned and is used by a small contracting firm, and has been well preserved.

Church Village Station, 29th August 1961.

D. G. Thomas

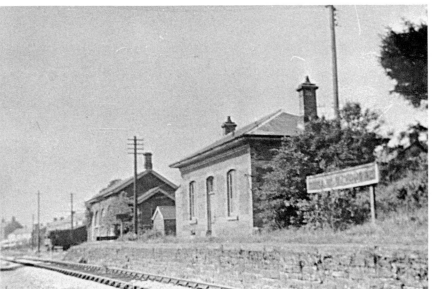

Llantwit Fardre Station, on 29th August 1961.

D.G. Thomas

Llantwit Station
Opened in January 1875, renamed Llantwit Fardre Station on 8th October 1936, closed for passenger services on 31st March 1952, and closed to goods traffic on 7th October 1963.

Llantwit Faadre Station, and Goods Shed, 1954

CB Swallow 028

Llantwit Fardre Station and Goods Shed, c1954.

Author's collection

Beddau Halt
Opened in July 1910 as Beddau Platform renamed as Beddau Halt on 1st October 1923, this halt closed on 31st March 1952. Today no trace of this halt remains, only the rail bridge is there while trees and grass now cover the whole area.

Cross Inn Station, 7th October 1961

G. Pearce

Cross Inn Station
Opened in January 1875, closed for passenger services on 31st March 1952, and closed to the handling of goods traffic on 9th May 1960. The station buildings are now used by a private car firm, the buildings are still in good condition.

Taff Vale Railway Cottage Sidings, as the name suggests, were situated next to the TVR built cottages at Maesaraul Junction. Today no trace is left, only an area covered with rough meadow grass marks the site, the sidings having been closed in February 1933.

Photograph showing the TVR cottages at Maesaraul Junction, the former sidings were the waste ground from where this photograph was taken, January 1985.

Author

Nos 5788 0-6-0PT and 4261 2-8-0T returning from Cwm Colliery with a Toad brakevan at Maesaraul Junction. The TVR line is on the left and the GWR line is on the right, with the TVR cottages in the background, 3rd May 1958.

S. Rickard

Llantrisant Station
Opened by the GWR in 1863, but running powers were granted to the Taff Vale Railway to allow connection with their Cowbridge Branch. Llantrisant TVR Station amalgamated with the GWR station for passenger services after the closure of goods traffic on 21st September 1925. Finally closed for passenger services on 2nd November 1964.

Llantrisant TVR Station, 1903.

Lens of Sutton

Llantrisant TVR Station, 1910.
Pontyclun Library

Llantrisant No.1 Branch, total length 7 miles, stretched from Common Branch Junction to Waterhill Junction. This was never used for passenger services, being opened to freight and mineral traffic on 11th September 1886. Closed on 28th September 1964. The location of the ground frames for goods sidings along this branch were at Cymric (sawmill), Croft-y-Guinea (general), Eagle Foundry (works), Creigau (quarry), Rhiw Saeson (general) and New Inn (general). Waterhall Siding closed to the handling of goods traffic on 13th July 1964.

Today a new housing estate is gradually taking over the former track at the Waterhall end of this long-closed branch.

Pannier tank No. 3403 coming off the Llantrisant No. 1 branch at Waterhall Junction, with the 1.15pm Creigau Quarries freight, 28th April 1964. The building behind the signal box is Waterhall Goods Depot.

D.G. Thomas

Llantrisant Common Branch ran from Common Branch Junction to Llantrisant Common Junction (connecting with the GWR, Ely Branch). Opened for freight and mineral traffic on 1st December 1863, today only the disused rail bridges show where this line once cut across the old Llantrisant Common.

GWR 0-6-2T No. 5601 climbing the bank out of Common Branch, 7th October 1961.
G. Pearce

Treferig Branch, consisted of single track, and started at Treferig Junction with the Llantrisant Common Branch, and finished at Glyn Colliery. This branch was opened to goods and mineral traffic in the April of 1883, and closed entirely in the early part of 1930. All that is left today is the bridge remains at Treferig Junction, located beside the Royal Mint at Talbot Green.

A very rare find – an envelope bearing the seal of the "Treferig Valley Railway, Secretary's Office".

B. Morris

Treferig Goods Sidings have changed beyond all recognition today, due to dense overgrowth, and the change of course of the river, which has turned the former track into a swamp in places. Much the same has happened to the former Castellau Sidings.

The Cowbridge Branch

The Llantrisant to Cowbridge line was opened as an independent railway, the Cowbridge Railway, in February 1865, for the handling of goods traffic, and for passenger services on 18th September 1865. This branch closed to goods traffic on 1st February 1965, having closed for passenger services on 26th November 1951.

No. 9780 0-6-0PT at Llanharry Station, 15th July 1959, facing towards Ystradowen.
H.C. Casserley

Llanharry Station opened in September 1865 and closed on 26th November 1951. Today the road bridge is still there, but all trace of the platforms has gone and a thick overgrowth covers this former station site.

Ystradowen Station

Opened in September 1865, and closed on 26th November 1951 for passenger services and to goods traffic on 9th May 1960. This site is now part of a timber firm and the only station remains being the derelict station master's house.

Ystradowen Station, c1900.

Lens of Sutton.

Trerhyngyll and Maendy Platform
Opened in the September of 1865 and closed for passenger services on 26th November 1951. The trackbed remains are still traceable, but all sign of this former halt has vanished long ago.

Trerhyngyll and Maendy Platform, photographed on 26th May 1959.
M. Hale

Aberthin Platform
Opened in September of 1865 and closed on 12th July 1920. The trackbed is still clearly visible and the TVR iron fencing posts are still in place along the track side, while gorse bushes cover the site of this former halt.

Aberthin Platform 26th May 1951.
M. Hale

Cowbridge Goods Station c1910.
Lens of Sutton

Cowbridge Goods Yard and Shed, 15th July 1951.

H.C. Casserley

Cowbridge Station

The original Cowbridge passenger terminal opened for passenger services on 18th September 1865. This service was then transferred to the new through station on 1st October 1892, thus the original station became used as a goods station. This finally closed on 1st February 1965, the second Cowbridge Station having closed for passenger services on 26th November 1951. The goods station buildings were dismantled on 27th June 1964 and today all traces of the goods and passenger stations have gone, and the area is now a housing estate.

During the Second World War, because of the fire risk from the bombing of Cardiff Docks, massive stocks of timber were transported and stored in Cowbridge Goods Yard.

Cowbridge Station and staff, c1921. Left to Right: Mr Lewis (porter), Mr Bishop (porter), Mr Bond (porter), unknown, unknown, unknown (driver), unknown (station master), Mr Jones (guard), Mr Crowley (guard) and Mr Legg (engineer).

Colin Chapman

A worthy send off for the last passenger service from Cowbridge Station on 26th November 1951. The crowd consisted of: Miss David (booking clerk), Mr Lewis (Ystradowen station master), Jack Bishop (porter), Matt Jones (platelayer), Daniel Punter (goods), Frank Willams (driver), Mr B. Thomas (bus inspector), Walter Carswell (platelayer), Mr Beer (guard) and at the top of the photograph Frank Golden and the Mayoress Mrs Florrie Hinton.

Miss David

Aberthaw Branch

The Cowbridge to Aberthaw Extension was opened to all traffic on 1st October 1892, but on 4th May 1926 until 11th July 1927 the passenger service between Cowbridge and Aberthaw was suspended. A move by the GWR to cut back in wastage, this branch finally closed to goods traffic on 1st November 1932, with passenger services ceasing on 5th May 1930.

St Hilary Platform closed on 12th July 1920, but re-opened by the GWR at a later date. Passenger services were eventually withdrawn on 5th May 1930 and freight traffic ceased on 1st November 1932. Today all that remains of this halt is the road bridge and the trackbed is slowly becoming a stream.

St Mary's Church Road Station closed to the handling of goods traffic on 1st November 1932 and passenger services on 5th May 1930. The remains of the TVR goods shed can still be seen, now used as a storage barn for hay. Also, most of the platforms and buildings are still in use and in fair condition, this former station now being in private hands, but it can be viewed quite easily from the road.

St Mary's Church Road Station, facing towards Llanbethery, photographed on 12th July 1959.

H.C. Casserley

Llanbethery Platform closed by the TVR on 12th July 1920 but re-opened and renamed as a Halt some time after the Grouping. It finally closed for passenger services on 5th May 1930, and to freight traffic on 1st November 1932. The road bridge is now the only remains that are to be seen, as it towers above this former site, half hidden amongst the dense overgrowth of trees and bushes.

St Athan Road Station, September, 1984.
Author

St Athan Road Station was temporarily closed for passenger services from 4th May 1926 until 11th July 1927, then re-opened. This station eventually closed for passenger services on 5th May 1930, and closed to the handling of freight traffic on 1st November 1932. Today the goods shed building can still be seen, also part of the platform and trackbed. The former station is also in the hands of a private firm. The abutments of the rail bridge (situated next to the station), which carried the Aberthaw line over the B4265 road, can still be seen.

Aberthaw Low Level Station
Opened on 1st October 1892 and known originally as Aberthaw Station, the Low Level suffix was added by the GWR on 1st July 1924. This station closed for passenger services on 5th May 1930 and to the handling of freight traffic on 1st November 1932. It is almost impossible to find the remains of this station now, only a small part of the platform remains can be seen through the tangle of ivy and undergrowth that has hidden the site. Snakes tend to warm themselves in the ashes and waste from the nearby Aberthaw Power Station and there is a sign situated at the far end, towards the harbour side, giving warning of their presence.

Aberthaw TVR Low Level remains photographed 21st October 1961.
D.G. Thomas

Aberthaw Lime and Pebble Company works, December 1984.
Author

End of the line: this branch ends at the site of the Aberthaw Lime and Pebble Works, which today is disused and neglected, although still an impressive sight.

Signal Boxes (and the men who worked them).

Llandaff Loop signal box, August 1985.

Author

A 'down' dmu passes Pentyrch Crossing signal box on 10th July 1959. This box closed in October 1962. The original Pentyrch Station building can be seen beyond the train.

S. Rickard

Walnut Tree Junction signal box at Taffs Well, 13th April 1968.

J. Morgan

Maesmawr signal box in 1975.

A. Powell

Approaching Treforest Junction signal box on 2nd May 1959 with the 12.45pm Clarence Road (former GWR station) to Pontypridd service. Photographed from an auto train hauled by 0-6-0PT No. 6438.

D. K. Jones

Pontypridd Junction signal box showing the Treherbert line on the left, and the Merthyr line on the right, c1968.

J. Morgan

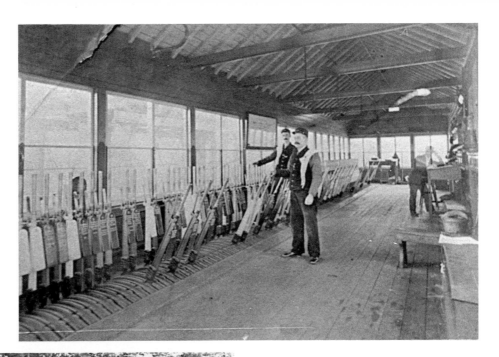

Pontypridd Junction signal box interior view c1904. There was a total of 135 levers.
P. Davies

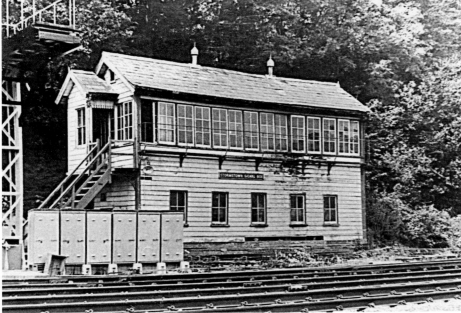

Stormstown signal box c1978, following closure on Sunday 4th September 1977.
D. K. Jones

Abercynon signal box on 3rd January 1964. Opened in 1932 to replace two former TVR signal boxes, Abercynon North and Abercynon South.

A. T. Miller collection

Black Lion signal box on 1st March 1968.
D. G. Thomas

Pontypridd Northern Junction signal box, with the main line on the left, Rhondda line on right and the Carmel Baptist Chapel in the distance. Photographed in the June of 1921.

B. J. Miller

Treherbert signal box, at the Blaenrhondda end of the station, photographed on 14th August 1954.

F. Hornby

Rhondda Fach Junction, North signal box, 8th July 1965.

D. G. Thomas

Gyfeillon Upper signal box (temporarily closed July 1983, taken out of use December 1984, dismantled October 1985). Photograph taken during December 1984.

Author

Signalman Richard Davies, passing the token at Cwmparc signal box, 7th May 1976. Closed March 1981.

J. Morgan

Pwllyrhebog signal box, situated at Tony-pandy, c1920.

C. W. Harris

Upper Bute Road signal box, Treorchy, c1900.

Rhondda Borough Libraries

Level crossing at Treorchy, looking north, c1900.

Rhondda Borough Libraries

National Colliery signal box (near Wattstown) closed December 1969. Photographed on the 13th April 1968, from a passing train.

J. Morgan

Roath Branch Junction signal box. Opened 1888, closed 1966 and demolished 1984 following use as a shunter's cabin. As seen on 1st April 1967.

D. G. Thomas

Penrhiwceiber signal box, upper side (GWR type) c1930.

Mr Jones

Nixons Crossing signal box, photographed 20th January 1968. This box was destroyed by fire in November 1985.
J. Morgan

Abercwmboi signal box, photographed in September 1970.
T.D. Chapman

Inside view of Abercwmboi signal box, showing the token machine for the line to Aberdare, c1975.
T. D. Chapman

Aberaman signal box c1910.
Cynon Borough Libraries

Ambrose William Pontin, born 1831, died 1907. The first signalman for the Taff Vale Railway, Aberdare Low Level Station. He also delivered telegrams and was the town constable.

P. Davies

Commercial Street Level Crossing, Aberdare North signal box, photographed during repairs, carried out to the crossing in 1963.

G. Davies

Radyr Quarry signal box, July 1983.

A. Powell

Interior of Radyr Quarry signal box, with signalman Gerald Morton, July 1983.
A. Powell

Grangetown signal box, 13th August 1966.
D. G. Thomas

Llandough signal box, 13th August 1966.
D. G. Thomas

Penarth Town signal box (closed May 1968), as seen on 4th May 1968.
J. Morgan

Penarth Cement Works signal box (closed May 1968), photographed on 15th August 1966.

D. G. Thomas

The former Lavernock signal box, seen here in the garden of this former TVR railway house, 4th April 1969.

D. G. Thomas

Sully signal box, circa 1922.
Welsh Folk Museum, St Fagans

Sully signal box, 23rd March 1957.
S. Rickard

TAFF VALE RAILWAY.

CARDIFF, *August 19th, 1900.*

SIR,

If you decide to come here in accordance with your application we will start you at work at once, and, if suitable, will place you on the Company's regular staff. The conditions of service of the various grades are as follow:—

Signalmen's wages vary from 20/- to 29/- per week, according to age and experience, with a bonus of £2, £3, or £4, according to the importance of the Box: £1 a year for boots: uniform supplied, including overcoat and leggings. Payment after 60 hours at overtime rate: time-and-a-quarter; Sunday duty stands by itself, and is paid for at the overtime rate: time-and-a-half for special Sunday duty.

Goods Guards (including Shunters) wages vary from 25 - to 31 - according to age and experience.

Brakesmen. Wages vary from 20/- to 23/- a week.

Guards receive cloth coat and vest, corduroy trousers, overcoats, leggings, sou'-westers, and 26/- a year boot money. Brakesmen receive cord suits, overcoats, leggings, sou'-westers, and 20/- per annum boot allowance.

Guards and Brakesmen are paid after 60 hours (which constitutes a week's work) at the rate of time-and-a-quarter. Sunday duty stands by itself and is paid for at the rate of time-and-a-half. All bonuses and boot money are paid half-yearly.

So that you may not come here under a wrong impression, I wish to state that the vacancies have been caused in consequence of the staff in the grades named having sent in their notices.

Ample arrangements will be made for the protection of men who come here for duty, and they will be provided with free quarters for the first fortnight, and for so long thereafter as the Company considers necessary.

Only those men who have had railway experience are required, there being many more applications from men who have not had such experience than there are vacancies for.

If you stay with us for three months we will repay you your fare to Cardiff.

Yours truly,

T. E. HARLAND,
Superintendent of the Line.

N.B. – Take your ticket to Cardiff (Great Western) Station; wire by what train you expect to arrive here, and you will be met on arrival by a Taff Vale Inspector in uniform, who will see that you are conducted to your lodgings. Do *not leave the Station with any other person.*

THE
AMALGAMATED SOCIETY OF RAILWAY SERVANTS.

OF
ENGLAND, IRELAND, SCOTLAND, & WALES.

Head Offices:—72, ACTON STREET, GRAYS INN ROAD, LONDON, W.C.

TELEGRAPHIC ADDRESS: "BEWARE." LONDON.

In reference to your [ ] Branch.

[handwritten notes]

AMALGAMATED SOCIETY OF RAILWAY SERVANTS

OF

ENGLAND, IRELAND, SCOTLAND, & WALES.

Head Offices:—72, ACTON STREET, GRAYS INN ROAD, LONDON, W.C.

TELEGRAPHIC ADDRESS: "BEWARE," LONDON.

_____ Brecon _____ Branch.

Address 4 St Michael Street Brecon

In reference to your [ ]

26 August 1900

Dear Sir

At a monthly meeting of this Branch held this afternoon the following resolution was unanimously agreed to:—

"That we the members of the Brecon Branch of the A.S.R.S. representing 96% of all grades of Railwaymen at and around Brecon unanimously resolve to support both Morally and Financially our fellow workers of the Taff Vale Railway in their firm stand for just rights of representation and we urge them to remain loyal to

to one and other"

Please convey the same to our Brothers of the T.V.R. and when you consent that they may receive outside financial support we shall be most glad to respond.

With personal sympathy for the men, and kind regards to yourself. I remain Dear Sir

Yours fraternally
W. H. Robbins
(Bor. Sec.)

Mr Bell
Gen Sec
A. S. R. S.

Cardiff

(155)

Telegram replies from other railway company employees offering their support to the TVR strikers in August 1900. (Reproduced with the approval of the National Union of Railwaymen.)

SLS special at Ynysybwl Station with the signal box in view, 11th July 1959.

S. Rickard

Cilfynydd signal box in a sad state, 2nd March 1968.

J. Morgan

Pont Shon Norton signal box, (closed 1970) on 1st November 1968.

J. Morgan

Cowbridge Road signal box (closed October 1983), 21st July 1961.

D. G. Thomas

The 10.50am auto train passing Llantrisant Common Branch Junction signal box in April 1934.
Courtesy the widow of the late H. Webber

Cowbridge signal box and staff, with a young Daniel Punter on far right. The photograph was taken in 1911, shortly after he joined the Taff Vale Railway Company.
Courtesy Mrs Harris, nee Beer

Railway Staff (Taff Vale and Great Western Railway years)

Taff Vale Railway horse drawn delivery wagon outside the Boot and Shoe exchange, in Market Street, Pontypridd c1906.
Pontypridd Library

Widows and Orphans Fund, Hopkinstown
TVR staff. These railway employees were
active charity workers for the widows and
orphans of railwaymen, around 1910.
Pontypridd Library

Taff Vale Railway female staff, employed
due to the lack of men created by the Great
War of 1914-1918.
Pontypridd Library

TVR staff at Pontypridd Station circa 1919.
Pontypridd Library

Pontypridd Goods Depot staff, c1924, in mixed TVR and GWR uniform dress.
Left to right, rear row: I. Phillips,
J. Davey,
H. Murley, F. Ferris,
F. Stearn, E. Reid,
C. Browne.
middle row: F. Roberts,
J. Eveis,
G. Coates,
D. Donovan,
H. Trembath,
H. Mansfield.
front row: W. Williams,
A. Morris,
W. Rees, Capt
A. Williams
(agent), A. Cress-well, P. Brennan
(foreman)
J.O. Farreh,
H. Richards
*(Names as recalled
by C. Browne)*
P. Davies

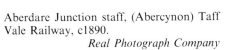

Aberdare Junction staff, (Abercynon) Taff
Vale Railway, c1890.
Real Photograph Company

TVR Staff from Hopkinstown, with de-corated float, c1920.
Pontypridd Library

Merthyr High Street station staff, 1945-1946 period.

Mrs M. Anthony

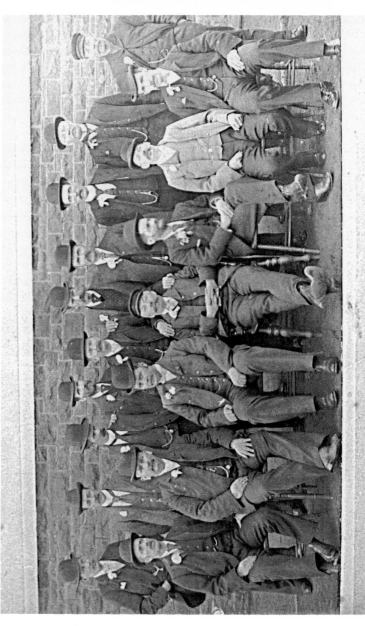

Helping Hand Fund, committee and staff from Treherbert TVR Station, c1910.

G. Coles

Treherbert Station staff, c1938.
Left to right: Bill Howard (guard), Eddie Griffiths (station foreman), Percy Knapman (guard), Dan Thomas (ticket collector), Bert Eastlake (guard), person unknown, George Foreman (guard), Bernie Roberts (station shunter), Stan Lewis (guard) and Bill Madocks (guard).
Courtesy of the widow of the late B. Eastlake

Collett 0-6-2T No. 5668, during V. J. day celebrations, at Treherbert engine shed, 1945. Left to right; David Evans (stores issuer), Alf James (engine driver), Ray Powell (fireman) and Malcolm Vaughan (fireman). Ray Powell was later to become a Member of Parliament and the locomotive is now preserved on the Pontypool & Blaenavon Railway.

G. Coles

Class O4, 0-6-2T No. 97 later renumbered by GWR as No. 298. Photograph taken in 1923 at Aberdare Low Level engine shed, with George Hinton (engine cleaner) on the right of the cab.

G. Hinton

Taff Vale Railway Company staff at Aberdare TVR Station, c1889.
Cynon Valley Libraries

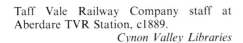

A faded photograph taken in c1910 of the surveyors contracted to supervise the erection of the new pontoon buildings at the TVR Company's Penarth Dock.

Associated British Ports

Penarth Town Station staff, c1930.
Left to right: Mr Winstone (ticket collector), person unknown, Alf Fry and Charlie Tooze (parcel porter).

F. Winstone

Llantrisant Station staff c1946. Mr Beer on far left, Mr Davies third from left.

Mrs Harris, née Beer

Taff Vale Railway staff at the first Cowbridge Station, photographed at the turn of the century. Second row, standing on right, Tom Bennet (signalman) and the seventh person standing from left is Mr Conway (guard).

G. Punter

TVR staff at Cowbridge Station, c1921.
Left to right rear row: Mr Legg (engine repairs), Mr Crowley (guard), Mr M. Jones (guard), Mr J. Bishop (porter), Mr Bond (porter), Mr Lewis (porter).
Sitting, front row: person unknown (booking clerk), Mr Williams (station master), Mr W. James (booking clerk), person unknown.

V. Bishop

Cowbridge Station c1930. Mr J. Bishop (porter) on the left with Mr Wilcox (guard).
V. Bishop

Procession of railway strikers, going to a general meeting. The crowd consists of Taff Vale and Barry railwaymen, members of the "Amalgamated Society of Union, and Railway Servants," Pontypridd, c1911. In the background, left, is a sign giving directions to the Barry Railway station at Pontypridd.

Pontypridd Library

Derailments and War Damage

Two photographs showing a derailment of Fernhill Colliery wagons at Treherbert, c1908.

Rhondda Borough Libraries

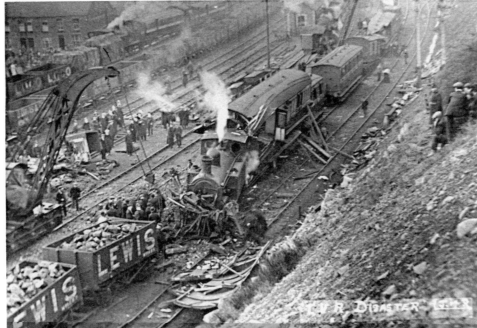

Three photographs of the TVR railway derailment at the Gyfeillon Coke Oven Works, near Pontypridd, at 9.45am on 23rd January 1911. A passenger train collided with a stationary mineral train, resulting in the death of twelve persons, and by a miracle the driver and fireman of the passenger train survived. The inquest which followed the derailment was held by the coroner Mr R. J. Rhys, and the jury was directed to return an open verdict.

Lens of Sutton and courtesy C.W. Harris

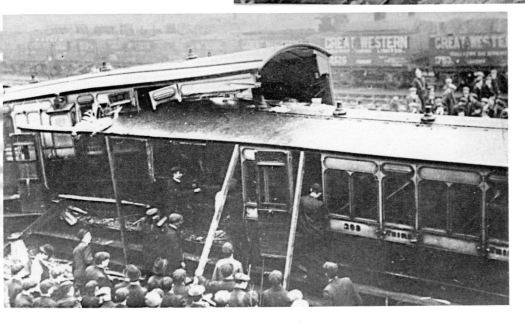

Derailment of coal wagons at Abercynon Station, c1910. The steep gradient from Abercynon Station was the cause of a runaway line of coal trucks which ended in a serious crash on the 'down' Merthyr line of the station.

B. Hamle

Derailment of runaway coal trucks, 14th June 1961 at Treherbert. A lot of damage was avoided when the one duty signalman spotted these runaways and diverted them into an empty siding. It was his actions that certainly saved railwaymen and the public from serious injury or even loss of life.
Courtesy the family of the late P. Gardener

Another runaway, this time on the Merthyr line, which ended up by demolishing the footbridge at Abercynon Station, May 1966. The photograph shows Abercynon Station staff with the derailment in the background.
Left to right: Mr W.M. McTravers (signal and telegraph department), person unknown, Mr J. Williams, Glyn Bennet and B. Noonan (guard).

Mr & Mrs Pugh

Merry-go-round coal wagons coming to an abrupt stop at Stormstown after running away near Lady Windsor Colliery, Ynysybwl, 14th May 1968.

A. Powell

Roath Dock, on the north side, heavy high explosive bomb damage to the rolling stock, permanent way and timber stocks, during the nights of raids on 3rd and 4th March 1941.

Associated British Ports/British Rail

TVR Cardiff West Yard Works c1926, showing the traverser.

Welsh Industrial and Maritime Museum/British Rail

Engines at Works, Yards and Sheds

Cardiff West Yard Works
Opened in 1840 these works were used for the building and repair of Taff Vale Railway locomotives until they were closed in 1926.

TVR 0-6-2Ts at Cardiff West Yard Works c1926.

Welsh Industrial and Maritime Museum/British Rail

Taff Vale Railway I class 4-4-0T No. 285, as rebuilt with larger boiler in 1914/15 and handed over to the GWR. Renumbered by the GWR as 1133, but still in TVR livery, it is seen in Cardiff Cathays shed, on 8th August 1924.

LCGB (Ken Nunn collection)

TVR 02 class 0-6-2T No. 84, renumbered as GWR 425, at Cathays shed on the 8th August 1924.

LCGB (Ken Nunn collection)

TVR No. 1, O4 class 0-6-2T, and others at Abercynon shed, c1922.

LCGB (Ken Nunn collection)

BR and GWR No. 337 at Abercynon shed, c1949. Originally TVR No. 10, an A class 0-6-2T, it was subsequently rebuilt at Swindon.

D.K. Jones

BR No. 194, photographed whilst shunting at Blaenclydach goods yard, Pwllyrhebog, on 21st June 1949.

This was one of three locomotives built for working the Pwllyrhebog Incline in 1884. Designated H class, these 0-6-0Ts were originally TVR Nos 141-143, GWR Nos 792-794 and BR Nos 193-195 respectively. No. 194 went to Swindon for scrap in 1954.

G.W. Sharpe

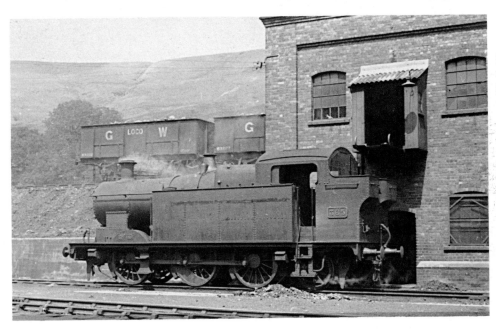

Former TVR A class 0-6-2T No. 130, now renumbered by GWR as 365, and seen here at the Treherbert coaling stage, 27th June 1938.

H.C. Casserley

Preservation

The Butetown Historic Railway Society Ltd, located in Bute Road, Cardiff, is run by voluntary donations and labour. Members are gradually improving this former TVR terminus, and eventually it is hoped that passengers will be carried to Queen Street Station and back.

Author

Taff Vale Coach Restoration at Brynteg Comprehensive School, Ewenny Road, Bridgend. At present this group is in the process of gradually and carefully restoring this former TVR brake coach No. 220, which was built in 1891. It is a massive task, but with donations and time, these boys will complete this excellent work.

Author

Welsh Industrial and Maritime Museum, Bute Road, Cardiff. This museum has in its grounds, a partly restored TVR coach which will one day take pride of place in the museum. This coach, which was built as TVR No. 48 in 1883, was rescued from Hayling Island, where it was used as a holiday home. Much of the work already done on this coach has only been possible through donations and it is with thanks to these people that one day we will see the complete restoration of this lovely vehicle.

Author

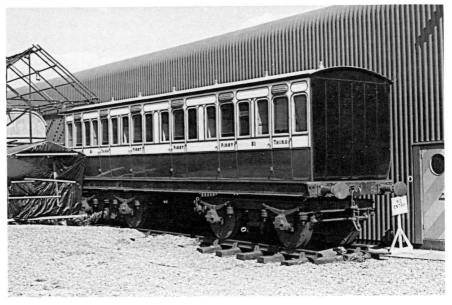

Caerphilly Railway Society, Van Roa
Caerphilly. This society has a very sma
part of the former Rhymney Railway wor
shops, but will, with the help of donatio
etc, hope one day to be able to purchase t
extra land at the rear of these former work
and thus to extend their track. At prese
they have TVR locomotive No. 28 O2 cla
0-6-2T on loan from the National Colle
tion, which has been fully restored an
remains a tribute to them and the Wels
Industrial and Maritime Museum. It is see
at th steam day held at Newport Station
August 1984.

Autho

Opposite bottom and above: Two views of former TVR 02 class 0-6-2T No. 85. Built by Neilson Reid in 1899 it later became GWR No. 426 and was sold for colliery use in the North East, becoming Lambton Hetton & Joicey Colliery Co. No. 52. It passed from the National Coal Board to the Keighley & Worth Valley Railway for preservation, where it has been a static exhibit until 1988. These photographs show it being pulled out of the museum in readiness for restoration to working order and rebuilding of its cab back to its original profile.

Both: Stuart Willets

Former GWR 2-8-0T No. 5227 is seen shortly after arrival at the Wales Railway Centre, under the newly constructed canopy, on 15th February. This locomotive was followed by another nine, all from Woodham Bros, Barry.

P.D. Nicholson

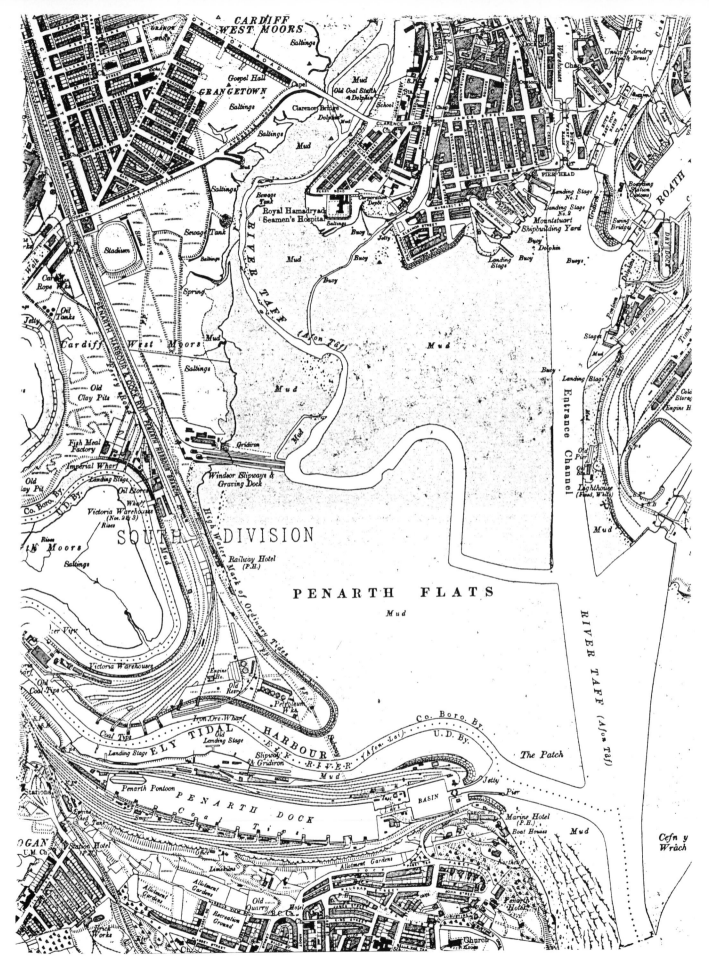

Penarth Dock area, reproduced from the Ordnance Survey map of 1922.

Llantrisant branch, reproduced from the Ordnance Survey map of 1921.

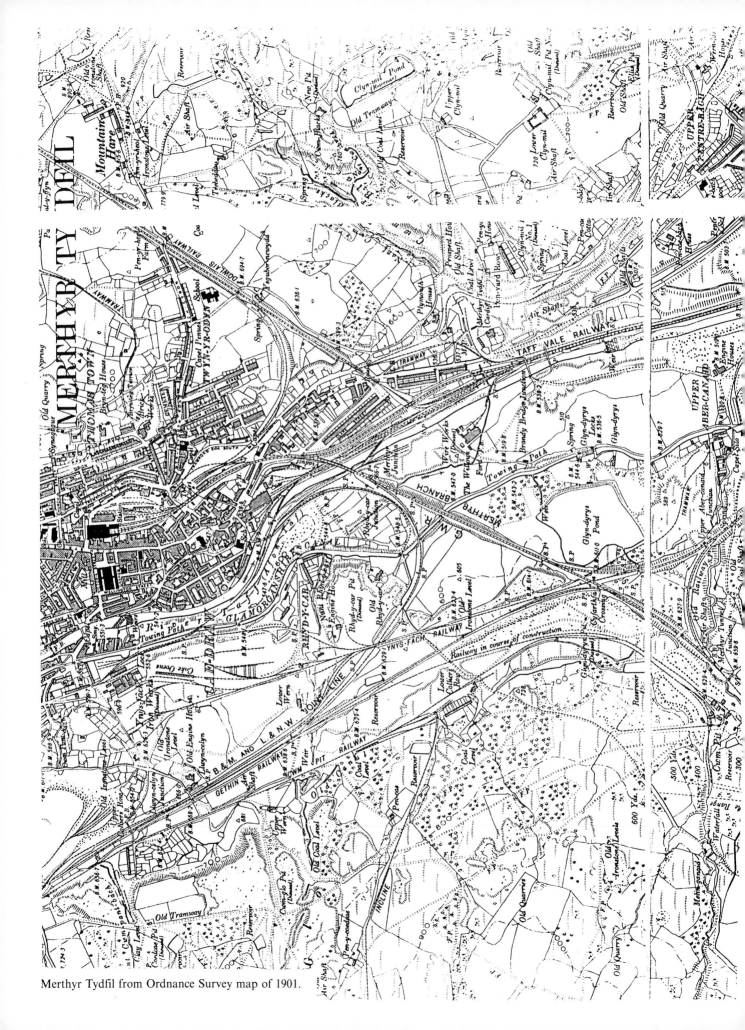

Merthyr Tydfil from Ordnance Survey map of 1901.

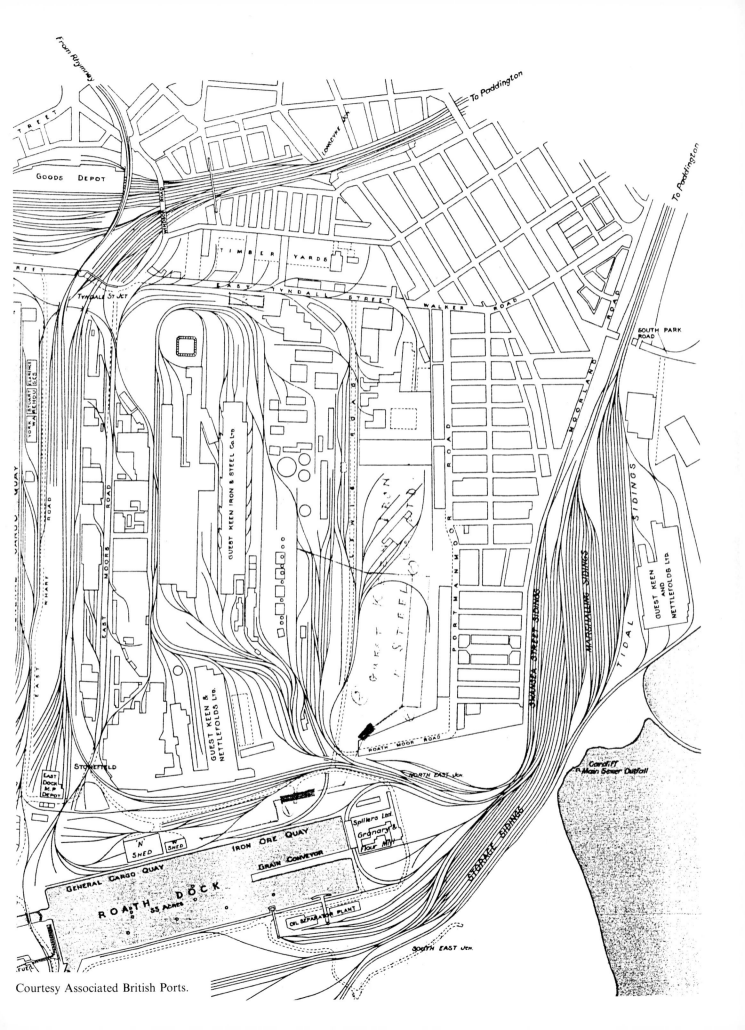

Courtesy Associated British Ports.

No. 10,106

TAFF VALE RAILWAY.

COAL STRIKE

SUPPLEMENTARY NOTICE OF ALTERATIONS IN PASSENGER, &c., TRAIN SERVICE.

Commencing on **MONDAY, APRIL 11th, 1921,** and until further notice, the following alterations must be brought into force, viz.:—

PASSENGER TRAINS DISCONTINUED (WEEK DAYS.)

UP.

5.48 a.m. Pontypridd to Nelson.
5.55 a.m. Pontypridd to Merthyr.
6. 4 a.m. Aberdare to Nantmelyn.
6.14 a.m. Mill Street to Nantmelyn.
6.32 a.m. Abercynon to Aberdare.
7.36 a.m. Aberthaw to Cowbridge.
7.45 a.m. Llantrisant to Pontypridd.
7.50 a.m. Penarth to Treherbert.
9.20 a.m. Cardiff to Pontypridd.
9.50 a.m. Pontypridd to Nelson **(Wednesdays).**
9.55 a.m. Pontypridd to Old Ynysybwl.
10. 1 a.m. Cowbridge to Pontypridd.
10.52 a.m. Pontypridd to Treherbert.
11. 0 a.m. Penarth to Clarence Road.
12.34 p.m. Pontypridd to Treherbert.
12.35 p.m. Pontypridd to Old Ynysybwl.
12.50 p.m. Porth to Maerdy.
1.14 p.m. Penarth to Riverside.
1.34 p.m. Pontypridd to Nelson.
2.32 p.m. Pontypridd to Merthyr (G.W.R.)
2.50 p.m. Abercynon to Aberdare.
2.50 p.m. Cardiff to Treherbert **(S.O.).**
3.38 p.m. Pontypridd to Old Ynysybwl.
3.40 p.m. Porth to Maerdy.
5.30 p.m. Quakers Yard to Merthyr, G.W.R. **(S.O.).**
7.15 p.m. Cardiff to Treherbert **(Thurs., Sats.).**
7.53 p.m. Pontypridd to Ynysybwl **(S.O.).**
8.30 p.m. Cowbridge to Pontypridd.
9. 5 p.m. Cardiff to Merthyr, G.W.R. **(Thurs., Sats.).**
9.26 p.m. Pontypridd to Old Ynysybwl **(S.O.).**
10.10 p.m. Penarth to Cardiff (Queen Street).
10.25 p.m. Pontypridd to Old Ynysybwl.
10.37 p.m. Mill Street to Nantmelyn.
10.40 p.m. Cardiff to Pontypridd.

Courtesy L. Lang

Brown & Sons (Seeds) Ltd.

ESTD 1845

DIRECTORS: J. BROWN J.A. BROWN

SEED AND BULB MERCHANTS

TELEPHONES
BRISTOL 23255/6

TELEGRAMS
"BROWN, BRISTOL"

BRIDGE STREET
BRISTOL, 1

22nd, March 1945.

Mr. F.S. Newman,
High Street,
COWBRIDGE.

THE GERMINATION AND PURITY OF THIS SEED IS EQUAL TO OR ABOVE THE STANDARD SPECIFIED IN THE TESTING OF SEEDS ACT, 1920

PER G.W.R. COWBRIDGE STN.   CARRIAGE Paid to Stn.   PACKED IN   2 bags.

			£	s	d
1½ cwt. Gladstone @ 21/- per cwt.			1	11	6
g 6d;				1	6
			21	13	-

1523

Brown & Sons (Seeds) Ltd
BRIDGE STREET,
BRISTOL, 1.
19 APR 1945   194

Received with thanks the sum of

£ 1 : 13 : -   Sig.

For Brown & Sons (Seeds) Ltd
19 APR 1945

IF ANY, REQUIRED TO BE GIVEN UNDER THE SEEDS ACT, 1920, WE GIVE NO WARRANTY EXPRESS
TOES OR SEED GRAIN SOLD BY US AND WE WILL NOT BE IN ANY WAY RESPONSIBLE FOR THE
N ACCEPTANCE OF THESE TERMS BY THE PURCHASER. IF THE PURCHASER DOES NOT ACCEPT

THE GOODS ON THESE TERMS THEY ARE AT ONCE TO BE RETURNED.

T.Y.R.

R(385)TA

A DAY at PENARTH

On MONDAY, AUGUST 29,

A DAY EXCURSION

WILL BE RUN TO

PENARTH

FROM	AT	RETURN FARES—3RD CLASS	
	A.M.	S.	D.
Maerdy	8 55	3	9
Ferndale	9 0	3	6
Tylorstown	9 5	3	3
Ynishir	9 10	3	0
Porth	9 20	3	0
Trehafod	9 25	2	9
Pontypridd	9 30	2	6
Treforest	9 35	2	3
Taffs Well	9 45	1	6
Radyr	9 50	1	3

The Return Train will leave PENARTH at 8.30 p.m. the same day.

Children under three years of age, free; three and under twelve, half-price. No luggage allowed.

Tickets may be obtained in advance at the Stations.

Excursion Tickets are only available to and from the Stations named upon them. Should an Excursion Ticket be used for any other Station than those named upon it, or by any other train than as specified above, it will be rendered void, and therefore the fare paid will be liable to forfeiture, and the full Ordinary fare will become chargeable. The tickets are not transferable.

CARDIFF, August, 1921.

E. A. PROSSER,
GENERAL MANAGER.

1,000 E 10280. 226500
WESTERN MAIL LTD. CARDIFF. 6810D.

TAFF VALE RAILWAY.

Parcels' Way-bill, No. *192* From Pontypridd Junction to *Llanishen* 19.19 Pro. No. *19.19*

(P.5.) Via *Q Yard*

10/30 o'clock Train, *Mar 29th* 188*7*

Waterlow and Sons Limited, Printers, London Wall, London.

Parcel	Description.	NAME.	ADDRESS.	Weight. Lbs.	Paid on. £ s. d.	To Pay £ s. d.	Paid. £ s. d.	Senders.
1 Pcl		J Fowler	Llanishen T.C.f.			2. 2.	Free	Agent
				TOTAL ...				

N.B.—The Guard of the Train must see that the Entries on this Bill correspond with the Parcels delivered to, and given up by him.

TAFF VALE RAILWAY AND RHYMNEY RAILWAY via PONTYPRIDD & CAERPHILLY.

	STATIONS.		a.m.	a.m.	p.m.	p.m.	
Taff Vale Railway.	Treherbert ... ... dep.		7 40	10 25	3 25	7 30	...
	Treorchy ... ... "		7 45	10 30	3 30	7 35	...
	Ystrad ... ... "		7 50	10 35	3 35	7 40	...
	Llwynypia ... ... "		7 55	10 40	3 40	7 45	...
	Dinas ... ... "		8 0	10 45	3 45	7 50	...
	Maerdy ... ... "		7 40	10 20	3 25	7 25	...
	Ferndale ... ... "		7 46	10 26	3 31	7 31	...
	Tylorstown ... ... "		7 52	10 32	3 37	7 37	...
	Ynishir ... ... "		7 57	10 37	3 42	7 42	...
	Porth ... ... "		8 7	10 51	3 52	7 57	...
	Hafod ... ... "		8 11	10 55	3 56	8 1	...
	Pontypridd ... ... arr.		8 16	11 0	4 1	8 6	...
G.W.R.	Pontypridd ... ... dep.		8 32	11 15	4 25	8 20	...
	Caerphilly ... ... arr.		8 45	11 28	4 38	8 33	...
	Newport ... ... "		9 20	12 0	5 10	9 5	...
Rhymney Railway.	Caerphilly ... ... dep.		9 8	12 45	5 35 7 43	9 30	...
	Penyrheol ... ... "		9 13	12 50	5 40 7 47	9 34	...
	Abertridwr ... ... "		9 19	12 56	5 45 7 52	9 40	...
	Senghenith ... ... arr.		9 23	1 0	5 50 7 56	9 45	...
	Caerphilly ... ... dep.		8 50	12 36	4 30	10 29	...
	Llanbradach ... ... "		8 56	12 43	4 37	10 49	...
	Ystrad Mynach ... ... "		9 4	12 50	4 43	10 46	...
	Hengoed Junction ... ... "		9 8	12 55	4 47	10 50	...
	Pengam ... ... "		9 13	12 59	4 52	10 55	...
	Bargoed ... ... "		9 21	1 5	4 58	11 0	...
	Brithdir ... ... "		9 26	1 9	5 2	11 4	...
	Tir Phil ... ... "		9 31	1 13	5 6	11 8	...
	Pontlottyn ... ... "		9 38	1 19	5 12	11 14	...
	Rhymney ... ... arr.		9 44	1 25	5 21	11 18	...

	STATIONS.		a.m.	a.m.	p.m.	p.m.	
Rhymney Railway.	Rhymney ... ... dep.		...	9 1	1§50	6 32	...
	Pontlottyn ... ... "		...	9 5	1§54	6 37	...
	Tir Phil ... ... "		...	9 11	1§59	6 43	...
	Brithdir ... ... "		...	9 15	2§ 3	6 48	...
	Bargoed ... ... "		...	9 20	2§ 8	6 55	...
	Pengam ... ... "		...	9 25	2§11	7 0	...
	Hengoed Junction ... ... "		...	9 32	2§16	7 6	...
	Ystrad Mynach ... ... "		...	9 35	2§21	7 12	...
	Llanbradach ... ... "		...	9 40	2§27	7 18	...
	Caerphilly ... ... arr.		...	9 46	2§33	7 24	...
	Senghenith ... ... dep.		...	9 27	2 5	6 5	...
	Abertridwr ... ... "		...	9 31	2 9	6 9	...
	Penyrheol ... ... "		...	9 36	2 14	6 14	...
	Caerphilly ... ... arr.		...	9 42	2 18	6 19	...
G.W.R.	Newport ... ... dep.		7 25	9 40	3 0	7 10	...
	Caerphilly ... ... "		7 57	10 12	3 32	7 42	...
	Pontypridd ... ... arr.		8 10	10 25	3 45	7 55	...
Taff Vale Railway.	Pontypridd ... ... dep.		8 36	10 32	4 10	8 3	...
	Hafod ... ... arr.		8 42	10 38	4 16	8 9	...
	Porth ... ... "		8 46	10 42	4 20	8 13	...
	Ynishir ... ... "		9 2	10 56	4 32	8 32	...
	Tylorstown ... ... "		9 8	11 2	4 38	8 38	...
	Ferndale ... ... "		9 14	11 8	4 44	8 44	...
	Maerdy ... ... "		9 22	12 2	4 52	8 52	...
	Dinas ... ... "		8 54	10 49	4 28	8 21	...
	Llwynypia ... ... "		9 0	10 55	4 34	8 27	...
	Ystrad ... ... "		9 6	11 1	4 40	8 33	...
	Treorchy ... ... "		9 12	11 7	4 46	8 39	...
	Treherbert ... ... "		9 16	11 11	4 50	8 43	...

For connecting trains to and from Swansea see pages 28 and 29. § Saturdays only.

Extract from TVR Timetable of July-September 1892.

26

WORKMEN'S TRAINS

Are run daily (except Sundays and Bank Holidays) as stated below :—

STATIONS.		Time.	FARES FOR THE DOUBLE JOURNEY.		
				WEEKLY	
			From Cardiff.	From Walnut Tree Bridge.	From Pontypridd.
		a.m.			
Cardiff (Queen Street)	... dep.	5 15			
Walnut Tree Bridge ...	{ arr.	5 28	1s. 6d.	......	......
	{ dep.	5 29			
Pontypridd	{ arr.	5 40	3s. 6d.	2s. 0d.	......
	{ dep.	5 45			
Hafod	,,	5 51	3s. 9d.	2s. 3d.	1s. 6d.
Porth	,,	5 54	3s. 9d.	2s. 3d.	1s. 6d.
Dinas	,,	6 1	4s. 0d.	2s. 6d.	2s. 0d.
Llwynpia	,,	6 6	4s. 0d.	2s. 9d.	2s. 3d.
Ystrad	,,	6 12	4s. 3d.	2s. 9d.	2s. 3d.
Treorchy	,,	6 17	4s. 6d.	3s. 0d.	2s. 6d.
Treherbert	,,	6 21	4s. 6d.	3s. 0d.	2s. 6d.

The tickets will only be available during the week in which they are issued (but not on Sundays and Bank Holidays) between the Stations named upon them, and by the trains shown in this bill; if used otherwise the full ordinary fares will be charged.

The tickets will be available on the return journey by the undermentioned trains only :—

STATIONS.		Except Bank Holidays and Saturdays.	Saturdays only.
		p.m.	p.m.
From ... Treherbert ...	...	5 10	1 30
Treorchy ...	...	5 16	1 35
Ystrad ...	...	5 20	1 40
Llwynpia ...	...	5 26	1 46
Dinas ...	...	5 31	1 51
Porth ...	...	5 36	1 56
Hafod ...	...	5 41	2 1
Arriving at Pontypridd ...	...	5 50	2 8
Walnut Tree Bridge ...	...	6 5	2 21
Cardiff (Queen Street)	...	6 18	2 33

No Luggage will be allowed by these trains except workmen's baskets of tools or food, which will be conveyed at owner's sole risk.

Third Class passengers may obtain ordinary tickets for the Up train at Cardiff (Queen Street), Walnut Tree Bridge and Pontypridd, and for the Down train at any of the Stations at which it calls.

27

Pic-nic or Pleasure and School Parties.

PIC-NIC TICKETS.

For Parties of not less than Six First Class, or Ten Second Class or Third Class Passengers, from and to Stations on this Railway, also, by arrangement, to Stations on other Railways, may be obtained at about a Single Fare and a Quarter for the Double Journey. They will not, under ordinary circumstances, be issued at a lower charge than 9d. for each Adult Passenger.

For distances of thirty miles and upwards, Parties of Thirty First Class or Fifty Third Class may travel at about a Single Fare for the Double Journey.

Application for Pic-Nic or Pleasure Party Tickets must be made in writing three clear days before the date of the proposed excursion, stating the following particulars :—

1. That the party is exclusively a Pleasure Party.
2. The probable number of the party.
3. The date of the intended excursion.
4. The Station from and to which, and the class of carriage for which tickets are required.
5. The trains by which the journeys will be made.

The right to refuse the granting of Cheap Tickets is reserved by the Company.

SCHOOL PARTIES.

Tickets at reduced fares are issued to parties of *bonâ fide* School Children and their Teachers; and, if the parties are sufficient in number, Special Trains will be run for their convenience.

Particulars of fares and arrangements for the conveyance of such Parties may be obtained from the Out-door Superintendent, Cardiff.

EXCURSIONS.

Excursion Trains will be run during the season to places of interest and in connection with special events at CHEAP FARES.

These arrangements will be duly announced by special bills.

MARKET TICKETS.

Cheap Market Tickets are issued at certain Stations to Cardiff, Pontypridd, Cowbridge, Merthyr, and Aberdare, on Market days.

For particulars of fares, &c., see bills at the stations.

The Butetown Historic Railway Society Wales Railway Centre

This society was started in 1977 with the purpose of building a workable and professionally run steam railway centre for enthusiasts, visitors and the inhabitants of the City of Cardiff. This would blend into the newly reorganised area of the former Cardiff Docks, and yet retain a piece of the past. The society started by restoring a very shoddy and almost derelict building that once was one of the Taff Vale Railway Company's most prized possessions. This is the terminus for passenger services to Cardiff Docks at Bute Road.

Although the identification of the Taff Vale Railway was not lost entirely at the Grouping in 1922, it became diluted with certain traditions from another great railway company, the Great Western Railway.

The history of the TVR terminus. This building was constructed in the early part of the 1840s and was the most southern terminus of the Taff Vale Railway, being used by the Railway as a head office from 1847 until 1862. In 1897 the TVR constructed a single platform at Bute Street Station, and eventually the original building was altered by the addition of extra rooms and bow windows, which quite enhanced the beauty of this building. The extension enabled a booking office and waiting rooms to be added, the redesigned station becoming known as Cardiff Docks. It was again renamed in 1926 as Cardiff Bute Road. The Butetown Historic Railway Society started the renovation programme on this derelict building in 1981. For quite a number of years previously it had been used as a storage warehouse.

Inside the building. Today, the downstairs rooms provide accommodation for the railway museum and congratulations must be given to the really excellent display of photographs on show. Also in this room, one can admire the excellent modelling work done by Mr Taylor of the Welsh Industrial and Maritime Museum, for his true-to-scale model of the area, showing the station, the TVR West Yard Works and the adjoining buildings along Bute Street, circa 1900.

In the other downstairs room is the art gallery and this display of many fine paintings comes under the expertise of Dr Stuart Owen-Jones, the Deputy Curator of the Welsh Industrial and Maritime Museum, Cardiff. Upstairs there is an efficient and well stocked cafe, which is just one of the renovated and fully restored rooms now used for lecturing and exhibitions, as well as modelling activities.

The station. The platform has been partitioned off from the running line, on the insistence of British Rail, which is quite understandable especially while locomotive restoration is in progress. Already a fair amount of welding has taken place, with the rubbing down and replacing of rusty parts. Secondly, the Society must protect its property from trespassers. Eventually when all has been achieved, an entrance will be provided for people, whether they be enthusiasts or just members of the public, as all will be welcome to taste the sense of achievement and nostalgia for the age of steam. This is something which can never be forgotten. This influx of sightseers will also be able to visit the other great attraction, situated a 100 yards southwards, the Welsh Industrial and Maritime Museum, and see the many exhibits and working engines there.

A new station canopy has been erected and covers some of the society exhibits. It was whilst the pillar foundations were being dug out that a small turntable was discovered, unfortunately damaged beyond repair. There is a lot of work to do, but much has already been achieved by this society under the auspices of the Wales Railway Centre. Eventually the ground owned by the society will cover an area of approximately 97,200 square feet. The first steps have already been taken to acquire the land needed to extend the concourse, refurbish the exterior and construct engine sheds based on the Victorian style. Between September and December of 1991 it is hoped to build another shed which will also be used for the protection of the carriages etc. Track laying and the other numerous schemes, such as a visitor's car park, should also be completed by the December of 1991, bringing the total expenditure to about two million pounds.

Locomotives. By the end of April 1988 the Society had twelve locomotives, including ten which had been moved from their sojourn at Mr Dai Woodham's scrapyard in Barry. Work is now in progress stripping the rusty plates and fittings from these engines and replacing these with renovated parts. These have joined the two original engines, *Sir Gomer,* a Peckett 0-6-0ST from Mountain Ash Colliery, and a North British built diesel shunter which formerly worked in East Moors Works, Cardiff. By December 1991, it is hoped to have around upwards of perhaps twenty locomotives in stock. There is also a community project run under the supervision of the probation services, with local youngsters from the Butetown area of Cardiff, helping to paint and restore the running stock, giving local interest and involvement.

Locomotives acquired for the Wales Railway Centre, February 1988.

BR No.	Former Co.	Designer	Built	Class	Type	Withdrawn	Cost to Society
2861	GWR	Churchward	6/18	2800	2-8-0	3/63	£9,000
4115	GWR	Collett	10/36	5101	2-6-2T	6/65	£6,000
5227	GWR	Collett	6/24	5205	2-8-0T	2/63	£6,500
5539	GWR	Collett	7/24	4575	2-6-2T	4/62	£5,250
6686	GWR	Collett	9/28	5600	0-6-2T	4/64	£5,750
7927†	BR	Collett	10/50	6959	4-6-0	12/65	£9,000
44901	LMSR	Stanier	10/45	5MT	4-6-0	10/65	£7,500
48518	LMSR	Stanier	8/44	8F	2-8-0	7/65	£7,500
80150	BR	Riddles	1/57	4MT	2-6-4T	10/65	£9,500
92245	BR	Riddles	11/58	9F	2-10-0	12/64	£10,000

† *Willington Hall*

Total £76,000

A present day listing of all traceable halts, stations, sidings and junctions situated on the main line and the branches, both used and disused, with the respective Ordnance Survey map references.

Main line

Cardiff West Yard Works	ST190748
Cardiff Bute Road Station	ST191748
Cardiff Queen Street Station	ST189765
Cathays Woodville Road Halt	ST181774
Maindy North Road Halt	ST175780
Cathays Carriage and Wagon Works	ST177778
Llandaff Station	ST148795
Radyr Station	ST135804
Pentyrch Crossing	ST129812
Pentyrch Station	ST129812
1st Taffs Well Station	ST129839
2nd Taffs Well Station	ST125832
Treforest Junction	ST083886
Treforest Goods Depot	ST083889
Treforest Station	ST083889
Pontypridd Station	ST072898
Northern Junction	ST070902
Pontypridd Goods Depot	ST079941
Abercynon Station	ST082947
Incline Top Station	ST089955
Quakers Yard Low Level Station	ST086965
Merthyr Vale Station	ST077995
Treod y Rhiw Station	ST071024
Pentrebach Station	SO070038
Brandy Bridge Junction	SO053051
Dowlais Junction	SO053053
Merthyr Junction	SO052054
Merthyr Plymouth Street Station	SO051056
Merthyr Viaduct	SO050060 to SO052055
Merthyr High Street Station	SO051061

Rhondda Branch

Rhondda Branch Junction	ST071901
Rhondda Cutting Junction	ST069902
Gyfeillon Halt	ST060907
Hafod Junction	ST048910
Trehafod Station	ST045910
Eirw (or Aerw) Branch Junction	ST042911
Porth Station	ST027913
Dinas Rhondda Station	ST006919
Tonypandy and Trealaw Station	SS998922
Pwllyrhebog Incline	SS993927 to SS981928
Blaenclydach (Pwllyrhebog) Goods Depot	(no trace)
Llwynypia Station	SS995938
Gelli Halt	SS980951
Ystrad Rhondda Station	SS973954
Pentra Halt	SS968958
Treorchy Goods Depot	SS961964
Treorchy Station	SS959965
Tylacoch Halt	SS957966
Treherbert Station	SS939981

Rhondda Fach Branch

Rhondda Fach Junction	ST916024
Porth Goods Station	ST025916
Ynyshir Station	ST025929
Wattstown Halt	ST022936
Wattstown Goods Station	ST019937
Pontygwaith Halt	ST012939
Tylorstown Station	ST010945
Ferndale Station	ST001973
Maerdy Station	SS975986

Aberdare Branch

Aberdare Junction	ST083948
Pontcynon Bridge Halt	ST078957
Mathewstown Halt	ST069968
Penrhiwceiber Low Level Station	ST062975
Mountain Ash Oxford Street Station	ST048992
Abercwmboi Halt	ST034997
Aberaman Station	SO013017
Aberdare Low Level Station	SO006026
Bwllfa Dare Branch	SO004028
(GWR) Dare Viaduct Foundations	SN992026
Aberdare Commercial Street	SO004027
Aberdare Mill Street Halt	SN998035

Ynysybwl Branch

Clydach Court Junction	ST082924
Clydach Court Halt	ST081925
Ynysybwl New Road Halt	ST065933
Robertstown Halt	ST063939
Ynysybwl Station	ST061943
Old Ynysybwl Halt	ST056950
Old Warehouse Sidings	ST048966

Llancaich Branch

Pont Shon Norton Junction	ST076911
1st Berw Road Halt	ST076911
2nd Berw Road Halt	ST077911
Coedpenmaen Station	ST082912
Cilfynydd Station	ST087924
Ynysdwr Junction	ST082940
Travellers Rest Station	ST084945
Llanfabon Road Halt	ST105951
Nelson Station	ST113954
Passing Loop Junction to Abercynon Colliery	ST084936 to ST082944
Stormstown Junction	ST079936
Stormstown Viaduct	ST081938
Llancaiach Line to Dowlais Cardiff Colliery (Abercynon)	ST081940 to ST082944

East Branch

East Junction	ST188761
Bute East Dock (West Side)	from ST191758 to ST194747
Bute West Dock (East Side)	from ST190757 to ST193747 (no trace)

Cowbridge Branch

Llanharry Station	ST018806
Ystrad Owen Station	ST014776
Trerhyngyll and Maendy	ST009766
Aberthin Platform	ST005756
Cowbridge Goods Station	SS999746
Cowbridge Station	ST000745

Aberthaw Branch

St Hilary Platform	ST011726
St Mary Church Station	ST020716
Llanbethery Platform	ST032694
St Athan Road Station	ST031678
Aberthaw Low Level Station	ST035665
Aberthaw Lime and Pebble Company	ST039662

Roath Branch

Roath Branch Junction	ST157792
Mynachdy Sidings	ST165791
Roath Depot Junction	ST200781
Roath Depot Sidings	ST204779
Roath Dock	ST205751 to ST200745

Penarth Branch

Radyr Sidings	ST137801
Penarth Junction	ST136803
Llandaff Loop	ST140795 to ST144796
Ely Fairwater Goods Shed	ST147773
Ninian Park Halt	ST167759
Penarth Curve North	ST170757

Sloper Sidings	ST171755
Penarth Curve South	ST173754
Canton TVR Goods Sidings	ST168759
Grangetown Station	ST175749
Llandough Halt	ST172731
Llandough Sidings	ST172733
Cogan Junction	ST175727
Penarth Tidal Harbour	ST180724 to ST188725
Penarth Dock Station	ST176725
Dingle Road Halt	ST181719
Penarth Town Station	ST185714

Cadoxton Branch

Alberta Place Halt	ST185707
Lower Penarth Halt	ST184698
Lavernock Halt	ST178686
Swanbridge Station	ST166680
Sully Station	ST152684
Biglis Goods Depot	ST143692
Biglis Junction	ST140692
Cadoxton Station Siding	ST133688

Llantrisant No. 1 Branch

Llantrisant No. 1 Branch Junction with Llantrisant Branch	ST059838
Llantrisant No. 1 Branch Junction with Common Branch	ST057836
Waterhall Goods Depot	ST143784
Waterhall Junction	ST144782

Llantrisant Branch

Llantrisant Branch Junction	ST094877
Tonteg Halt	ST098867
Church Village Station	ST086858
Llantwit Station	ST075850
Beddau Halt	ST067841
Llantrisant Junction with Common Branch	ST059838
Cross Inn Station	ST056831
Maesaraul Junction with GWR Mwyndy Branch	ST052826
Cottage Sidings	ST053827
Llantrisant Sidings	ST035815
Llantrisant TVR Station	ST035815

Llantrisant Common Branch

Llantrisant Common Branch Junction with Ely GWR Branch	ST028848
Llantrisant Common Branch Junction with Llantrisant Branch	ST059838
Llantrisant Common Branch Junction with Llantrisant No. 1 Branch	ST057836

Treferig Branch

Treferig Branch Junction	ST043850
Treferig Goods Sidings	ST034874 (approx. area)
Castellau Goods Sidings	ST045862 (approx. area)

NB. Treferig and Castellau heavily changed due to dense overgrowth and the overflow of water from the river.

Additional Halts

Cathays (British Rail)	ST182773
Treforest Industrial Estate (GWR)	ST107862

Acknowledgements

Grateful acknowledgement is due to the following for their help and time, and for the use of their prints and photographs which have made this book possible.

Thanks go to all the people who made me welcome in their homes and at their places of work and helped me with information and photographs. Also, to my good friend Alun Powell, 'A Radyr Man' for his help and to the photographers both amateur and professional who must have stood almost on the same spots that I have, as without their help or foresight there would be no past on record. Also to the ex-employees of the Taff Vale Railway, as well as the Great Western Railway, and the former and working employees of British Railways, who must have seen the same sights I have, but perhaps in better and happier times.

Mrs M. Anthony, Merthyr.
Associated British Ports.
Aberdare Reference Library.
Mr S. Bailey, Chairman, Butetown Historic Railway Society.
Mr N.L. Browne, Surrey.
Mr B. Brooksbank, London.
Mr V. Bishop, Cowbridge.
British Rail.
Branch Line Society.
Brynteg School Railway Group.
Butetown Historic Railway Society Ltd.
BRSA, Merthyr Branch staff & members.
BRSA, Cardiff Branch staff & members.
Mr A. Burton, Aberdare.
Mr Buttigieg of Powell Duffryn Wagon Co.
Mr C. Batstone, Pentre.
BBC Manchester
Mr B. Broadstock, Abercynon.
Barry Preservation Society.
Cynon Valley Libraries.
Mr V. Crabb, Pontypridd.
Caerphilly Railway Society.
Mr T.D. Chapman, Cardiff.
Mr R.J. Caston, Newport.
Mr G. Coles, Tynewydd.
Caerphilly Local History Society.
Cowbridge District Local History Society.
Cynon Valley History Society.
Mr C. Chapman, Daventry.
Mr H.C. Casserley, Berkhamstead.
Cardiff Reference Library.
Mr P. Davies, Pontypridd.
Dowlais Reference Library.
Miss B. David, Cowbridge.
Mr G. Davies, Aberdare.

Mr J. Dore-Dennis, Westra.
Dinas Powis Local History Society.
Mr M. Davies of BRSA Merthyr.
Mr Evans, Nelson.
Mrs Eveliegh of Cowbridge Museum.
Mr Francis, Arts Officer Merthyr Library.
The Glamorgan County Archives Office.
Mr R. Gulliver, Whitby.
Glamorgan Rail Users Federation, Cardiff.
South Glamorgan Libraries.
Mr M. Grant, Cardiff.
The GWR Museum, Swindon.
Mr M. Hale, Dudley.
Mr C.W. Harris, Porth.
Mrs B. Harris (nee Beer), Cowbridge.
Mr F. Hornby, Surrey.
Mr B. Hamlet, Abercynon.
Mr G. Hinton, Pontypridd.
Mr C. Hughes, Abercynon.
Mr J. Hunt, Trelewis.
Mr D.K. Jones, Mountain Ash
Mr A. Jones, Rhondda Museum.
Mr P. Korrison, St Albans.
Mr A. Keir of Roath Local History Society.
Mr J. Knapp of the National Union of Railwaymen.
Miss M.E. Loveridge, Penarth.
Lens of Sutton.
LCGB (Ken Nunn collection).
LGRP/David & Charles Publishers Group.
Mrs Lewis (nee White), Tonpentra, Rhondda.
Mr W. Lightfoot, Pencoed.
Mr R. Linsley of British Railway Board.
Mr K.A. Ladbury, Salisbury.
Mr L. Lang, Efail Isaf.
Llantwit Major Local History Society.

Mr A.T. Miller, Huntingdon.
Mr. H. Morgan, Cowbridge.
Merthyr Tydfil Historical Society.
Mid Glamorgan County Libraries.
Mr J. Morgan, Cardiff.
Mr B.J. Miller, Barry.
Merthyr Tydfil Public Libraries.
Mr B. Morris, Merthyr Tydfil.
Merthyr Tydfil Heritage Trust.
Mr M. Morton-Lloyd.
Mountain Ash Library.
Mr J. Murphy, Cardiff.
Mr T. McCarthy, Gilfach Bargoed.
Merthyr Express Newspaper.
Mr P.D. Nicholson, Shepton Mallet.
National Museum of Wales, Cardiff.
Mr P.R. Newman, Cowbridge.
Dr E.S. Owen-Jones of the Welsh Industrial and Maritime Museum, Cardiff.
The Ordnance Survey Department, Southampton.
Practical Model Railways.
Mr R. Powell, MP, House of Commons, London.
Mr H. Poulton AMEE, Cathays, British Rail.
Pontypridd Reference Library.
Penarth Reference Library.
Mr G. Punter, Cowbridge.
Penarth Times Newspaper.
Pontypridd Observer Newspaper.
Mr Pugh and Family, Abercynon.
Mr R. Phillips, Nelson.
Mr G. Pearce, Grangetown, Cardiff.
Penarth History Society.
Pontypridd Historical Society.
Mr J.B. Phelps of Associated British Ports.
Mr E. Perkins, Grangetown, Cardiff.
Mr B. Phillips, Caerphilly.

Railway Club of Wales.
Mr R.C. Riley, Beckenham.
Rhondda Borough Libraries.
Mr S. Rickard, Bishopbriggs, Glasgow.
Rudry Local History Group.
Railnews Newspaper.
Real Photographs Co, Ian Allan Ltd.
Mr J. Rees, Ynysybwl.
Mr G.W. Sharpe, Barnsley.
Dr E. Scourfield, Sully.
Mr N. Sprinks, former PR officer, British Rail.
Mr R. Strange, SRRS of Nottingham.
Sully History Society.
Mr R. Steer, Abercanaid.
Steam Railway Record Society.
Mr A.A. Smith, Merthyr Tydfil.
Mr P.W. Semmens of N.R.M, York.
South Wales Echo Newspaper.
Jessop of Leicester Ltd.
Mr C. Tagholme of British Rail, Swindon.
Tonypandy Library.
Mr Tilt of the Signalling Record Society.
Mr D.G. Thomas, London.
Mr H. Thomas, Pontypridd.
Treorchy Reference Library.
Mr D. Watkins, Merthyr Tydfil.
Mr R. Wilding, Pontypridd.
Warwickshire University, Modern Records Centre.
Welsh Railway Research Circle.
Welsh Folk Museum, St Fagans, Cardiff.
Westrail Enterprises Limited.
Mr N. Watts of Associated British Ports.
Mr C. Williams, Abercynon.
Mr F. Winstone, Penarth.

Also a special thank you to the following:-
To the widow of the late Mr C.R. Clinker, and the publishers Avon Anglia, who gave permission to use the notes from his Register of Closed Halts and Stations.
The widow of the late Mr H. Webber, for the use of his photographs that were taken during the late 1930s.
The widow of the late Mr B. Eastlake, for the use of the photograph of the Treherbert Railway staff.
The family of the late Mrs M. Griffiths, a grand old lady.
The family of the late Mr D. Proudley, a good friend.
The family of the late Mr P. Gardener, for the help and the use of their father's excellent photographs.

To the publishers David & Charles, for permission to use notes from their Regional History of Great Britain, Vol.12, an excellent work by Mr D.S.M. Barrie, and I would also like to thank Oakwood Press for their kind permission in allowing the use of material from The Taff Vale Railway also written by Mr D.S.M. Barrie, especially the references to the opening dates of the Stations, Halts and Branches.
To Mr N. Bell formerly of Oxford Publishing Company for his help and guidance and also to the two persons, who did a lot of work for me during the early stages of my research, Mrs M. Werret and Mr D. Miller.